D1440998

VICTOR EMMANUEL II

Victor Emmanuel II

and the Union of Italy

C. S. Forester

Simon Publications
2001

Copyright © 1927 by C. S. Forester

First published by Methuen & Co. Ltd. London

Library of Congress Control Number: 27015076

ISBN: 1-931541-77-9

Published by Simon Publications, P. O. Box 321, Safety
Harbor, FL 34695

CONTENTS

LIST OF ILLUSTRATIONS

THE HOUSE OF SAVOY

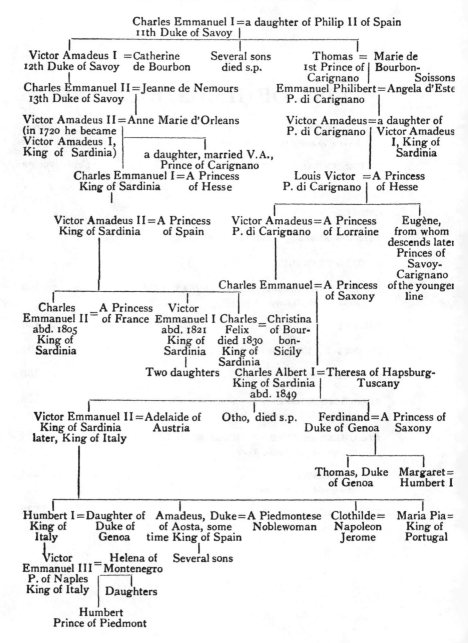

Charles Emmanuel I = a daughter of Philip II of Spain
11th Duke of Savoy

Victor Amadeus I = Catherine   Several sons   Thomas = Marie de
12th Duke of Savoy   de Bourbon   died s.p.   1st Prince of | Bourbon-
                                                Carignano | Soissons

Charles Emmanuel II = Jeanne de Nemours   Emmanuel Philibert = Angela d'Este
13th Duke of Savoy   P. di Carignano

Victor Amadeus II = Anne Marie d'Orleans   Victor Amadeus = a daughter of
(in 1720 he became   P. di Carignano | Victor Amadeus
Victor Amadeus I, | I, King of
King of Sardinia)   a daughter, married V.A., | Sardinia
                       Prince of Carignano

Charles Emmanuel I = A Princess   Louis Victor = A Princess
King of Sardinia   of Hesse   P. di Carignano | of Hesse

Victor Amadeus II = A Princess   Victor Amadeus = A Princess   Eugène,
King of Sardinia   of Spain   P. di Carignano   of Lorraine from whom
                                                                  descends later
                                                                  Princes of
                                                                  Savoy-
                                                                  Carignano
                   Charles Emmanuel = A Princess   of the younger
                                       of Saxony   line

Charles   = A Princess   Victor
Emmanuel II   of France   Emmanuel I Charles _ Christina
abd. 1805   abd. 1821   Felix = of Bour-
King of   King of   died 1830 bon-
Sardinia   Sardinia   King of   Sicily
                                      Sardinia
            Two daughters   Charles Albert I = Theresa of Hapsburg-
                             King of Sardinia | Tuscany
                             abd. 1849

Victor Emmanuel II = Adelaide of   Otho, died s.p.   Ferdinand = A Princess of
King of Sardinia   Austria   Duke of Genoa   Saxony
later, King of Italy

                                    Thomas, Duke   Margaret =
                                     of Genoa   Humbert I

Humbert I = Daughter of   Amadeus, Duke = A Piedmontese   Clothilde =   Maria Pia =
King of   Duke of   of Aosta, some Noblewoman   Napoleon   King of
Italy   Genoa   time King of Spain   Jerome   Portugal

Victor   = Helena of   Several sons
Emmanuel III Montenegro
P. of Naples
King of Italy | Daughters

    Humbert
Prince of Piedmont

VICTOR EMMANUEL II
AND THE UNION OF ITALY

CHAPTER I

ITALY AFTER THE CONGRESS OF VIENNA

" IN the beginning was the Word " and there was little else. There was no Italy. For the matter of that, there had never been any Italy since the days of Theodoric the Goth. All through the middle ages Emperors had been crowned Kings of Italy, but the Italy over which they reigned was only a fraction of the peninsula, and though they reigned they most certainly did not rule. The cities of the valley of the Po owed the Emperors a nominal allegiance; so did those of the Romagna; but the Popes vehemently denied that the Emperors were their feudal overlords; and Naples and Sicily, although for a short time they were the personal appanage of the Emperors, and indeed the main source of the power of some of them, soon broke aloof and settled down to furious dynastic struggles between Angevins and Aragonese, tempered and varied by armed interference by Popes and Saracens. The Italy over which the Emperors reigned hardly comprised more than Lombardy and Tuscany, and of Tuscany the most important part—the city of Florence—early won independence.

Then the Visconti were granted the duchy of Milan; the Medici slowly laid hold of the dominion of Tuscany; Venice turned her attention to the conquest of the mainland; Naples achieved virtual independence under her bastard Aragonese dynasty; for a brief while Italy was ruled by Italians, though not by an Italian.

But the unstable state of affairs was bound to end, and end it did, mainly through the machinations of the Sforza who had succeeded the Visconti. The Barbarians—French, German, Spaniards—poured into the unhappy peninsula. Italy was looted from end to end. Even Rome itself was pillaged by the Constable de Bourbon and his masterless mercenaries. The glory, the comparative freedom, the wealth of Italy passed like a dream. Naples, Sicily, and Lombardy fell to the crown of Spain. The Medici still held Florence, but their very title of Grand Dukes of Tuscany showed the change that had taken place. The States of the Church were solid and extensive—thanks mainly to Cæsar Borgia's conquest of Romagna—but the misgovernment of the Papal States was already developing into a byword. Genoa and Venice still retained their freedom, but their glory was departing with the discovery of the new routes to India, the conquest of the New World, and the fall of the Empire of the East. The petty dukedoms of Parma and Modena were utterly subservient to Spain. Only in the extreme north-west, where the House of Savoy had gained a foothold in Piedmont, was there any glimmer of hope—and not much there.

For two hundred and fifty years the situation hardly altered. Lombardy, reduced by cessions to Piedmont, passed to Austria. A younger line of the Spanish Bourbons obtained Naples and Sicily, and there set up an independent Kingdom, after Sicily had for a few years passed to Piedmont. Sardinia came to be looked upon as an integral part of Italy after its cession to the House of Savoy. Otherwise, Italy had no history. Utter inertia had descended upon the country.

Then came the French Revolution—and Napoleon. In ten years the work of as many centuries appeared to be undone. Piedmont, Tuscany, Parma, Modena, Venice, even Rome, changed masters. The western half of Italy was united to France, and Rome became the second city of the French Empire. Venice, having been flung to Austria as a bribe for her compliance with the treaty of Campo Formio, passed under French domination after Austerlitz. Once more the valley of the Po became an Emperor's Kingdom of Italy— Lombardy and Venice, welded together, giving the title of King to Napoleon. But under the Emperor of the French the lamp of liberty burned no more brightly than it had done during the previous two centuries. The ancient republics of Genoa and Venice were wiped out; Napoleon was a less responsible monarch even than the old despots—for he could if necessary bring army corps of Frenchmen to put down any popular movement against him. The press was muzzled; compulsory military service was made universal; the Continental system was enforced with the utmost rigour; and in addition Napoleon changed about at whim the crowned deputies whom he established in various parts of Italy. He drove out the Neapolitan Bourbons from Naples in 1806, and set up Joseph Bonaparte. Transferring Joseph to Spain, in 1808, he replaced him by Murat. Once there had been a Kingdom of Etruria, with a Bourbon as monarch. Two years later it became a part of France, under a governor-general who was one of his sisters. To suggest a union of the whole peninsula was treason, and was treated as such. With sublime contempt for any such enlightened ideas, Napoleon hacked off little fragments of Italy—Reggio, Taranto, Benevento, Ponte Corvo, Lucca, and dozens of others—and made presents of them to his ministers and marshals, although even he took care to arrange the transfers with a suddenness that took the wretched inhabitants unawares, so that they could not present petitions or raise objections to this arbitrary method of procedure.

That is the dark side of Napoleon's rule of Italy. But there is a brighter side which more than balances it. Napoleon might be a despot, but he was at least an orderly despot, and moreover the very conditions under which he had grasped power led him to establish his despotism on a foundation unheard of before in the annals of despotism—a foundation of legal equality. The feudal system, whose bad points had survived for centuries after its good ones had become inefficacious, was utterly swept away. The corvée, the unbearable game laws, the dues and the fines, went the way of " benefit of clergy " and seignorial mills. Equality, actual as well as fictitious, in the eyes of the law, became universal. A civil service at once efficient, economical, and just, saw that the weighty public burdens were no more weighty than was necessary. Prompt justice saw to it that brigandage was put down—even if the justice was sometimes quite untempered with mercy. Murat's ferocious lieutenant, Manhes, adorned every mile of the main roads of the Kingdom of Naples with heads and limbs, but every head and every limb had once belonged to a malefactor. Despite the cruel drain of recruits for the army, which fought France's battles in Russia and Germany and Austria and Spain, Italy prospered and flourished as she had never done since the Renaissance. Yet perhaps when all is said and done, the greatest gifts which Napoleon brought to Italy were the ones whose effect could be least easily measured—the revival of the term " the Kingdom of Italy " and the gift to the Kingdom of a national flag.

After Napoleon fell, and after Murat's double or triple treachery had ended in his having to face the firing party at Pizzo, the Congress of Vienna set itself deliberately to the task of effacing the memory of Napoleon and all his works throughout Italy. To Austria was given, actually and theoretically, the overlordship of the whole country. Austria had had to make concessions elsewhere, yielding up the Austrian Netherlands, and confirming Bavaria and Würtemburg in the territories they had wrung from her as the price of deserting Napoleon, so that in the eyes of the Congress of Vienna it was only fair that she should receive compensation on her south-western frontier. Venice and Lombardy were placed under the immediate rule of Francis I, who became now King of Lombardo-Venetia as well as Emperor of Austria, King of Hungary, King of Bohemia, and Duke and Count of half a hundred other territories. The other historic republic of Italy—Genoa—fell to Savoy. Metternich and the Holy Alliance could not stomach the idea of a Republic anywhere in Europe. Besides, it was necessary to reward the King of Sardinia for the constancy of his opposition to Napoleon. True, he had not always been so constant—he had made in 1796 the armistice of Cherasco which had been the first prominent achievement of the young Bonaparte —but ever since then he had continued in arms against the French. Even this could hardly be considered surprising, seeing that all his continental possessions—nine-tenths of his population and nineteen-twentieths of his revenue—had been seized by them. But now he had Genoa as a reward; besides, the Congress of Vienna was not averse to building up a strong state on France's south-eastern frontier, as it had done on her north-eastern.

Tuscany was restored to its dynasty of the younger line of Hapsburg-Lorraine. This dynasty had had more vicissitudes of late than any other. Tuscany had come into the family in exchange for Lorraine at the period of the Seven Years' War;

when Napoleon seized upon Florence he compensated the ruler with a duchy in Germany, carved out of ecclesiastical domains and attached to the confederation of the Rhine, and then he had changed its frontiers about almost monthly to agree with his varying policy in Germany. In 1814 the duchy was scrambled for by Bavaria and Austria. For a brief space there was some talk of giving it to Eugène de Beauharnais, Napoleon's stepson and late Viceroy of Italy, but no European power could rise to such heights of altruism. The duchy fell to Bavaria, but the family of Hapsburg-Lorraine was set up in Tuscany once more in compensation.

In Parma no such restoration was at once possible. The Parmese Bourbons would have to wait for a while. They might have been constant or they might not. It was inconstancy that the Congress of Vienna had to reward at present. Marie Louise, Napoleon's second Empress, had enabled the Allies to escape from an awkward situation when she had deserted her husband and thrown herself into the arms of Count Neipperg. She had saved the Emperor of Austria from having to dethrone his own daughter; she had brought with her her son—the hope of the Bonapartist party, so that they would not have to trust him to dangerous companions such as his father; she had smirched the name of Bonaparte in the eyes of all Europe; it was even believed that she had betrayed her husband's plans before she had blotched his honour. Services such as these must needs be rewarded, and only a sovereignty would be adequate. So Marie Louise was set up as Grand Duchess of Parma, with Neipperg, her paramour, as Prime Minister and Commander-in-Chief. Happily, any offspring from the union would be illegitimate, and if the couple were to marry after Napoleon's death (as indeed they did) the subsequent children would be morganatic. The Parmese Bourbons would only have to wait until Marie Louise's death before they would come into their own again. Meanwhile, Lucca was detached from Parma and set up as an independent principality for their benefit.

The Papal States were re-erected just as they had stood before the cataclysm. Pius had bowed in the house of Rimmon, had crowned the usurper in Paris, but he had repented in time. He had been robbed of his territory, cast into prison at Savona, and in reply had flung out bulls of excommunication which had damaged Napoleon's cause not a little. And Louis of France looked with a kindly eye on the re-establishment of the Papal power; so did Spain; so did Naples; and however much Austria coveted Romagna to round off the Kingdom of Lombardo-Venetia she could not possess herself of it in the face of such opposition.

Of the condition of the Papal States it is sufficient at present only to say that to be a State servant it was necessary to be a priest; there was almost a system by which one could only be a governor of a town or hold some other high rank in the State provided one was a bishop—and most of the executive heads were cardinals. Confusion in State affairs was practically certain while this condition prevailed, and when it is borne in mind that the clergy at this epoch had been large sufferers financially under the Napoleonic régime, it must be realized that there was no State in Europe so utterly reactionary as that ruled by the Pope. Which is saying a great deal.

The condition of the Two Sicilies was at first a little better. Murat's vigorous rule had brought order into Naples, where never order had been before. In 1815 the finances were in a strong position, for although the Napoleonic wars (and Murat's profusion) had cost a great deal of money, the greater part of this was owed to France, and the debt was repudiated on the return of the Neapolitan

Bourbons. All through the Napoleonic wars, Sicily had remained in Bourbon hands—even the Straits of Messina were wide enough to keep back Napoleon —and with the protection of a British fleet had come the installation of a British Minister, Bentinck, who was almost a British governor, by whose influence wholesale reforms had been made in the civil service and in the constitution. What was equally important, was that the continual bickering between Murat and the Bourbons had done much to rid Sicily of her bad characters; these had been landed in droves on Neapolitan territory by that militant churchman, Cardinal Ruffo, and, thanks to Manhes' prompt measures, now mouldered in quarters at the milestones on the Neapolitan roads. Between Ruffo and Manhes, Murat and Bentinck, Sicily and Naples were for the moment in a condition of order and prosperity which had never been approached since the days of the Romans, and which has hardly been approached since. Yet the Bourbons were installed, on Murat's fall, as Kings of the Two Sicilies. They were given a free hand to root out all the promise of the present state of affairs. Why, is not quite clear. It was the Austrians—Marie Louise's Neipperg at their head—who beat Murat, even though it was the Bourbons who shot him. After that, Naples had to go to somebody, so that all memory of the Napoleonic régime in Italy could be blotted out, and it was the Bourbons who had ruled it nine years ago. The Bourbons rushed their forces into the peninsula, and annexed Naples from under the noses of Neipperg's triumphant Austrians. Then what with being in possession, and being able to plead the divine law of " legitimacy," they were in too strong a position for Austria to meddle.

It was a *coup* characteristic of the Neapolitan Bourbons. They were always ready and prepared to snap up unconsidered trifles. They had cast longing eyes on Malta, on the Balearic Islands, on

Umbria.   When the Peninsular War broke out a young prince of the house arrived at Gibraltar.   As the King of Spain and the heir apparent were in Napoleon's hands there was just a chance that there would be a vacancy for him—and he had come on that chance.   His presence was hugely embarrassing. The English Governor did not know what to do with him.   The Spanish Juntas did not want to have anything to do with him.   But in faction-torn assemblies like the Juntas he was sure of finding someone to support him.   It took the united efforts of the Governor, of the Juntas, and of Wellington himself, commanding in chief the British army, to induce him to go away and worry someone else.   Most probably it was as well that he went.   The Juntas were hard enough to deal with, as Wellington found to his cost.   A Neapolitan Bourbon Prince of two-and-twenty would have been even worse.   It might be the climate; it might be effect of tradition, but every dynasty that had held the sovereignty of the Two Sicilies had degenerated appallingly.   The Norman rulers had done so; so had the Angevins; so had the Aragonese. The names of the two Joannas of Naples were proverbial for treacherous and depraved actions. Naples had been the grave of the Hohenstaufens— even Nelson had wandered from the strait path of justice during his stay there.   And the Bourbons were no exceptions to this rule—not by any means.

The only other independent State of Italy unmentioned so far was Modena, the smallest of them all, and very possibly the most unhappy.   The Duke of Modena was a Hapsburg like his neighbour of Tuscany, but he was more than a Hapsburg.   He was a Hapsburg-Este, for an Austrian Archduke had married the heiress of the one remaining native Italian house, and to his son had descended not only the sovereignty of Modena but the huge estates of the Este family.   To him also had descended the ingenious temperament of the Italian tyrants of the Renaissance period—an intolerant bearing towards anything popular (in the political sense), a cold cunning in the matter of intrigue, and a brutal ferocity towards wrongdoers that distinguished him even above his " dear cousin " of the Two Sicilies.

So Italy was divided, parcelled out among a crowd of alien families, overshadowed by the might of Austria, with no history save for the shadowy memories of Napoleon's reforms and of his red, white and green flag, and with, apparently, as little future. Yet already, in 1815, there were plans and schemes for the uniting of Italy. Murat had dreamed the wild dream—and the dream came to an end when he faced the firing party at Pizzo. There were vague talkers who hoped that it might come to pass, and who did little to bring it about. But at the moment the mass of the people were too concerned with other wrongs to think of anything so high-flown.

Far removed from the mass of the people there were other schemers, however, who also played with the idea. True, the idea of using a popular movement to gain their ends would have seemed to them not only blank folly but the blackest treason to their order. For they were the rulers of Italy, and they designed to unite Italy in the good old medieval fashion by means of dynastic marriages. The centre of stress was Savoy. The House of Savoy seemed to be coming to an end in the male line. The end of the direct line was indeed inevitable and close at hand. To succeed was only the young Prince of Carignano, whose ancestry had diverged from the main line some generations before. But the last of the ruling dynasty had two daughters. Maria Theresa, Queen of Sardinia, combining Italian talent for intrigue with the traditional policy of her native Hapsburg house, married them, the one to the Grand Duke of Tuscany, the other to the Duke of Modena. There seemed a chance of a powerful State being formed by peaceful means in Northern Italy. But the chance remained a chance and no more. Charles Felix of Sardinia had to give way to circumstances beyond his control and arrange for the succession of the Prince of Carignano.

And, too, it soon became apparent that Italy would never be allowed to work out her own destiny in peace. Within six years of the abdication of Napoleon, Austria interfered in the domestic policy of Italy. She was to continue in that armed interference for another forty.

Upon Italy had descended her twin plagues—priests and police. The country began to seethe with discontent through the inefficiency of the governments and the savagery and corruption of the police. Education and public works were at a standstill. The jealous despots watched for any word that might be considered to be disrespectful of despotism, and offenders were flung into prison without trial and kept there during the royal pleasure.

The monarchs were bound in secret agreement to Austria never to allow the slightest trace of constitutionalism to appear in the territories they ruled, and this was the sort of agreement to which even Italian monarchs adhered. But it was not merely constitutional slavery, nor was it desire for union, which caused the early outbreaks in Italy. They were purely the result of misgovernment. After five years of Ferdinand's rule in Naples the populace began to chafe. The secret society of the Carbonari, whose activities had been great under Murat, fanned the embers into a blaze. There was a sudden rising of the people, at first more or less orderly, and characterized by a flow of petitions demanding mild reforms. But active revolt, unless carefully handled, has a way of developing rapidly and passing beyond control. From reform in the government the people passed to demand reform in the constitution. The army was to be employed to chastise any such sacrilege, but the army was full of Carbonari. Then a divisional commander, General Pepe, proclaimed his Carbonarism, and twenty thousand soldiers joined in the demand for a constitution. It was high time for concessions, if Ferdinand wished to retain his throne. With this alternative before him no one was more lavish in promises than Ferdinand. He promised a constitution, he promised reform, he abolished taxes on the necessaries of life. In a few days he had apparently passed from rabid despotism to pure liberalism.

The movement was not viewed with favour by Ferdinand's brother-despots. The Powers hurriedly called a conference. England's moderating influence and Alexander of Russia's half-hearted sympathy were set at naught by Metternich's cold-hearted diplomacy. Then the representatives of the Powers met at Laybach. They would hear of no negotiations with the " rebels." They would only deal direct with the King. Nothing was more easy. Ferdinand took a fresh oath to the constitution, installed his son as regent, and, accompanied by the blessings and the prayers of his subjects, hurried off to Laybach. Here he implored Austrian interference, which was only too readily granted, and, with Sardinia, Tuscany and Parma all applauding, thirty thousand Austrian troops violated Papal neutrality by marching into Naples, won a couple of scrambling battles, and drowned the revolution in blood. A few hundred persons were condemned to death; a hundred thousand were listed by the police as suspect, and nothing more was heard of the constitution from Ferdinand, after he had abrogated it.

A similar, but unconnected, rising had occurred in Piedmont. There the King, Victor Emmanuel I, had actually abdicated, appointing his young and supposedly Liberal cousin, the Prince of Carignano, Regent. The Prince promised much—a free press, a Liberal constitution, State reform—in fact, he gave even more than was asked of him. Unfortunately, it was too good to be true. A warning voice came from Modena, where was Charles Felix, Duke of Genoa, Victor Emmanuel's brother and now king as a result of the abdication. He denied any responsibility for the Prince's actions, and boldly announced that he would insist upon untempered despotism. Behind the denial was the naked threat of Austrian bayonets; and the Sardinians, divided between the loyalty they so strangely felt towards their King, and their oaths to the Carbonari, could not organize resistance. The insurrection petered out, and Charles Felix entered Turin as a permanent and unbridled despot.

The troops of Austria were poured into the length and breadth of Italy. Armies of occupation kept Naples and the Duchies quiet, and were paid by the wretched populaces upon whom they were inflicted. Priests and police settled down to their life's work of misruling Rome and tormenting the peasantry. For a few years a blight of inaction spread over the land.

It passed slowly. The Papal States gradually developed a condition of permanent unrest. It was hardly to be wondered at, and sometimes the unrest became so pronounced that Austrian troops were called in again to calm the people with a few shootings and hangings. Sicily began to display a marked hatred for the Bourbons, and, what was more disconcerting, an unwonted tendency to united action. Usually Sicilian rulers could count on putting down one faction by the aid of another, on playing off Palermo against Messina, but now this was becoming impossible. The Bourbons could still rely, however, upon Neapolitan troops when used against Sicily, and perhaps on Sicilians against Neapolitans.

One or two heroic actions throw the general inaction of these few years into higher relief. The Bandiera brothers with sixteen men tried to conquer Naples, very naturally failed, and were equally naturally shot. Sicily rose against the Bourbons, and was put down with a cynical disregard for the laws of humanity—armistices were broken, amnesties ignored, towns sacked, and a pretty taste in wholesale execution displayed.

But in general Italy, to the superficial observer, lay idle, stagnating. The menace of Austria lay across the land, and to this menace was added a new one, equally threatening, for Louis Philippe of France appeared upon the scene, displaying a desperate anxiety to play a part in the drama, out-Austrianing the Austrians in his determination to maintain the Pope on the throne of his predecessors, while his quaint regard for the " legitimate " claims of the despots contrasted curiously with the circumstances under which he had come to power. Italy was thoroughly repressed, and the forces that were working against the repression were divided in their objects. Some wished merely for reform, some for definitely constitutional reform. Some sought to establish a republic, some a democratic monarchy. Some sought to unite Italy into a confederation on the Swiss model, and a few—a very few—wanted to unite Italy under one King. For anything to come of all these diverse tendencies two new factors were needed. One was a new impetus, and another was a focus. The new impetus came, as it inevitably would. But first it is necessary to examine the beginnings of the focussing of Italian unrest in the North.

CHAPTER II

THE HOUSE OF SAVOY

OF all the reigning houses of Europe, hardly one could compare in antiquity of origin and in length of pedigree with that of Savoy. The Bourbons could look back to Hugh Capet, and the House of Hanover to William the Conqueror, and, perhaps, through the female line, to the Saxon Kings, to Cerdic, and to a legendary descent from Wodin. But the male line of William had died out centuries ago, and the male line of Hugh Capet was now dispossessed and languishing in Styria while a younger branch occupied the uneasy throne. Except for these two, the other families of Europe were parvenus in comparison with Savoy. Hapsburgs, Hohenzollerns, Wittelsbachs, Würtembergs, had been still unknown at a time when the House of Savoy flourished.

The sovereignty dated from the grant by the Emperor to Umberto of the White Hand of the county of Savoy in 1034. Less than thirty years afterwards his successor had extended his dominions by a convenient marriage, and Savoy had gone on increasing ever since. Sometimes it was by a marriage, sometimes by opportune treachery, sometimes by sheer hard fighting. Peter of Savoy had given a young cousin of his in marriage to Henry III of England, and had been rewarded by the Earldom of Richmond, a substantial pension, and a manor on the banks of the Thames to which he gave his name, and which in turn has given names to theatres,

15

hotels, and a series of comic operas. One Duke became Pope; another secured Nice; most of them from time to time secured scraps of Piedmontese territory.

The family had its vicissitudes, of course. All the time that it was gaining in Italy, it was losing in Burgundy, where France was slowly advancing towards the Alps and the Rhine. But its gains were more than its losses. One Duke came into violent collision with the Swiss, and nearly experienced the fate of Charles the Bold of Burgundy. Another, Emmanuel Philibert, saw his whole State overrun by the French, and was reduced to earning his bread as a mercenary in the employ of Spain. But the family were good soldiers—they would not have survived so long had they not been—and Emmanuel Philibert won back all and more than he had lost by gaining for Philip II the victory of St. Quentin, which Motley ranks along with Crécy and Agincourt. For this he was re-established in his dominions, and licensed to plunge once more into the turmoil of Italian politics and catch what he could. The eternal struggles between France, Spain and Austria gave the Dukes of Savoy opportunities innumerable. By good fortune and deft policy they managed to change sides in each war just in time to find themselves on the side of the eventual victors, and were proportionately rewarded. The War of the Spanish Succession brought them their biggest prize, Sicily, but an unkind fate and unsympathetic Powers tore it from them seven years afterwards, giving in return only the poor consolation of Sardinia.

From Counts of Savoy they had become Dukes of Savoy; from Dukes of Savoy they had become Kings of Sardinia. They were still anxious for more. There was a painful interlude during the Napoleonic wars, when the troops of Savoy were routed, and Savoy, Nice, and all Piedmont became parts of France, but that was amply compensated for by the granting of Genoa to the Kingdom at the general peace. Victor Emmanuel I, to whom this prize was granted, tried hard to secure Lombardy as well, but Austria was too strong for him. The treaties of Vienna left the Kingdom of Sardinia a powerful, compact little State on both sides of the Alps, with a tradition of expansion southwards, a loyal nobility and a talented dynasty, and a future— the future was not as clear as it might be.

Individually, the heads of the house displayed marked characteristics. They were good soldiers and sound diplomatists. One or two of them had led saintly lives, but these were very much exceptions to the general rule. As far as the statement can be reconciled with the foregoing, they were devout Catholics. They were masterful, they would brook no interference with their privileges or their power, and they were as hot-tempered and as precipitant as was compatible with good diplomacy. The people they ruled made good soldiers, and were very largely devoted to their rulers. But at the beginning of the century they were not very interested in Italian affairs in general, for the simple reason that they did not consider themselves Italians. In the case of the Savoyards this was undoubtedly true, and the Piedmontese had been Frenchmen for nearly twenty years up to 1814. They differed in dialect from other Italians, and to some extent they differed in race.

The government of Piedmont was a benevolent despotism—at least as benevolent as the Jesuits would allow it to be. Corruption was not so rampant in government circles as it was in the rest of the peninsula, although certain evils arose from the feuds that were prevalent between the various noble families. Education was in the hands of the priests, and certain subjects could only be taught by Jesuits. Under these conditions, aggravated by a severe restriction of the press, the general standard of

B

education was low, although the university students, here as everywhere else in Italy, formed a turbulent nucleus of comparative intellectuals.

But on the whole the government was good; moreover, it was firm, and it rested on a solid basis of tradition and of affection. The Kingdom of Piedmont was the happiest part of Italy.

By 1820 it was clear that the direct line of Savoy was coming to an end. Victor Emmanuel I had no sons, nor had his only brother, Charles Felix, Duke of Genoa. The succession would pass in course of time to the house of Savoy-Carignano, which traced its descent from a son of Charles Emmanuel I, the husband of the daughter of Philip II of Spain.

And the representative of this line, the future heir to the throne, was destined to be first the most important, and then the least important, man in Italy. He was to be hailed as the saviour of Italy, and he was to be scorned as a failure. He was to be cursed as a traitor. He was to be called, pityingly, in after years, the Hamlet of Italy. Sometimes he was to let " I dare not " wait upon " I would," and sometimes he was to plunge rashly where wiser men would have been more cautious. Nowadays Charles Albert is known mainly as the father of Victor Emmanuel II, but upon him in his time as much as upon his son did the fate of millions depend.

He had started a little unfortunately. When the King of Sardinia retired before Napoleon to the island whence he drew his title, Charles Albert, Prince of Carignano, was left behind as a mere child. He passed into the wardship of Napoleon, was made a Count of the Empire of the French, and in consequence he had become tainted, in the opinion of his pharisaical royal cousins, with the evils which Napoleon personified. He was sixteen only at the restoration.

Princes of a younger line occupy a peculiar

position in monarchies. Any movement against the monarch invariably tries to increase in apparent importance by enlisting their aid. And they, when they try to move against the monarch, can generally rely on the support of some part of the people. In English history this is in evidence time and again. Simon de Montfort was Henry III's brother-in-law; the Lancaster who rebelled against Edward II was Edward's cousin; Richard II's cousin Henry headed the movement against him; even William of Orange was James II's nephew and son-in-law. In the same way in France at the beginning of the Revolution the Liberals were backed by Philippe Égalité—who, indeed, stood in much the same relationship to Louis XVI as did Charles Albert to Victor Emmanuel I.

It was inevitable, considering both this relationship and his past, that Charles Albert should be drawn into contact with the reforming party in Sardinia. After the revolt in Naples in 1820, the reformers became more active than ever. The Carbonari had branches all over Piedmont, and it was darkly whispered that the Prince of Carignano was a Carbonaro, too. In 1821 the reformers rose, the trouble starting, as usual, in a students' riot. Victor Emmanuel I lost his head—figuratively speaking. He had no intention of losing it in fact. He would not grant the constitution demanded, and when he found his troops hesitating he got himself out of the difficulty by abdicating. The heir to the throne, his brother, was absent at Modena, and so the regency passed naturally to the next heir, Charles Albert. Charles Albert was now twenty-three. He was undoubtedly in sympathy with the reformers, and also it appeared to him that the reason why the regency had been given to him was so that he might grant a constitution. He granted one, and he granted much more. Then came Charles Felix, King of Sardinia, and at his back fifty thousand

Austrian troops. The rebellion collapsed, and
Charles Felix disavowed all his cousin's actions,
punished the rebels, and re-established himself as an
absolute monarch. He settled down to a policy
of severe, almost savage, repression, and worse than
all, Charles Albert abetted him.

His destiny was in the hands of the King. A
word from Charles Felix might have sent him to the
scaffold. Even if he were pardoned, his succession
to the throne was none too secure. The daughters
of Victor Emmanuel had married Italian princes,
and it would not have been extraordinary if it were
announced that after Charles Felix the next King
of Sardinia was to be Francis of Modena. Perhaps
Charles Albert was honestly sorry that he had
misinterpreted the wishes of his family by granting
the constitution. He may have done the latter
against his will. However it was, he gave his
countenance to Charles Felix's campaign of
repression, and thereby blotted his scutcheon indelibly
in the eyes of the people. Thereby, too, he broke
his oath as a Carbonaro—if ever he had been one.

He had to prove to Charles Felix that his
repentance was sincere. He went into exile, and
joined a typically legitimist crusade—the French
campaign of 1823 against the Spanish constitu-
tionalists. When he came back, he signed an
agreement promising that when he reached the
throne he would make no alteration in the
constitution to which various bishops and the Order
of the Annunciation did not agree. In consideration
of this Charles Felix signed a will leaving him the
crown, and the whole affair ended in 1831 by Charles
Albert's succeeding to the throne pledged to
maintain autocracy at all costs. There can be no
denying that at some period he had promised the
exact opposite, either definitely or by implication (by
his actions during his brief regency). Whatever
happened, and whether he would be able to govern

his future actions by his own free will or whether any course of action were forced upon him, there would be for certain some section of the people who would believe him a traitor and a perjurer. It would be a severe handicap to the strongest man—to Charles Albert it was simply crippling.

But before all this trouble started, there had appeared upon the scenes the man who was to cut the Gordian knot, to whom Italy was to be indebted both for unity and for representative government, the Moses who was to lead the people out of bondage. At the moment he was a boy of eleven, and he had received the title of Duke of Savoy when his father, Charles Albert, became King of Sardinia. He was the eldest child of his father, by his wife Theresa, Archduchess of Austria. And he had been christened Victor Emmanuel.

Charles Albert came to the throne in an atmosphere of distrust. The nobles did not like him —he had been a democrat once. The people did not like him—he was now an autocrat. The Austrians did not like him, and their dislike was more dangerous than the hatred of other parties. For once upon a time Charles Albert had unbosomed himself to his Grand-Ducal father-in-law of a scheme —one of many—which he had evolved. He had proposed the union of Italy in a confederation, of which the Austrian Emperor's kingdom of Lombardo-Venetia would be a member, and of which the Austrian Emperor would be President. But this last gilding of the pill was not sufficient to conceal from the Emperor the fact that it *was* a pill. For were Italy a confederation, it might well take upon itself the business of interfering with the domestic affairs of each of its members, and the domestic affairs of Lombardy and Venetia would not bear interference. But, more important than this, the formation of the confederation would set men's minds thinking about a more definite union—and the

Emperor could be sure that he would have no part in a united Italy. Lost would be his Italian provinces; lost his unbounded influence throughout the rest of the peninsula. Affairs in Germany were none too promising. He did not wish to have a powerful potential enemy in the South as well. But the fact that Charles Albert had broached the scheme showed the direction in which his thoughts were tending, and from that day he was suspect in the eyes of the Empire. It is only one example of the wild carelessness which Charles Albert displayed all his life.

At the time of his accession Charles Albert made it plain that he was to be a benevolent despot. He strengthened the censorship of the press, hanged and imprisoned a few people who paid no attention to this regulation, and he struck fiercely at anybody who suggested either representative government or a union of Italy.

For by 1831 many people were thinking of the union. Why they were obnoxious to the King was because they proposed the wrong kind of union. They wanted republics, and confederation with the Pope, and they called for plebiscites and all sorts of dangerous arrangements. If anyone had proposed that Italy should be united by one of the only two means which a despot could tolerate—dynastic marriages or conquest—and had put forward a practicable suggestion how to carry it through, Charles Albert would have been delighted, so long as it was the house of Savoy which was to benefit. He would have no objection to extending his autocratic rule throughout Italy. But no one had so far thought of this.

The man who was the moving spirit in the republican idea was Giuseppe Mazzini. He was Genoese, one of Charles Albert's subjects, which made it all the worse. He wanted republics everywhere. The union of Italy was secondary. No republic would be tolerated unless it were strong enough to fight the Holy Alliance, and only all Italy combined would have any hope of this. So he began to conspire. He founded a rascally society— rascally in Charles Albert's opinion—which embodied in the first two articles of its constitution the need for the destructon of all the governments in Italy and the establishment of an Italian republic. To Charles Albert this was simple treason. To an equally influential potentate it was more than treason, it was heresy and blasphemy. For the Pope sincerely believed that it was essential to the Christian faith that the Head of the Church, the Vicar of Christ, should be possessed of temporal power—in other words that he should be in a position in which he could be conspired against, and in which he would have to devote more time to the physical needs of his million or so of subjects than to the spiritual needs of all the hundred million Christians in the world.

So the priests flung themselves into the task of persuading Charles Albert that Mazzini's Young Italy should be rooted out. He required little persuasion. He was horrified at the news that such a society should exist. Mazzini escaped—he was fortunate. The hangman dealt with his followers, and Mazzini was left to wander through Europe a penniless conspirator. And since in the eyes of the greater part of the world a republican was as obnoxious as a communist is now, Mazzini was doomed to a life of misery. But he established himself in London in the end, where he gained the friendship of the Carlyles, and whence he poured forth a continuous stream of exhortation and advice. Along with his exhortation he occasionally sent instructions for risings, but Mazzini was the worst practical conspirator in history. He could not plan a rebellion—he was too much of a dreamer—and if the freedom of Italy had depended on him alone the country would still be under Austrian dominion and still supporting Bourbons and Hapsburgs. Fortunately he found a practical revolutionist at hand in the person of Garibaldi, who, after one experience of the feebleness of Mazzini's organizing power, took upon himself the direction of military affairs, leaving to Mazzini the business of propaganda. Propaganda was Mazzini's forte, and the stream of appeals which he poured forth bore excellent fruit. It was almost entirely due to Mazzini that a large proportion of the population of Italy came to realize that salvation lay through the union of Italy, and that little reform was possible until union was achieved.

So Italy went on. In Lombardy and Venice the people suffered under an Austrian dominion as brutal as it was alien. In Modena and Parma they bore a heavy yoke of pure misgovernment. In the Papal States they endured priestly rule. In Naples they were condemned to bear all the disadvantages of their fellow-Italians and a few others peculiar to the country. But the seed sown by Mazzini and many other propagandists was beginning to bear fruit, and, more important than anything else, some of the people were looking to the Kingdom of Sardinia to relieve them of their troubles. Why this should be so, seeing that Sardinia was ruled by a renegade who was the fiercest despot of them all, is a matter that will bear analysis.

Charles Albert and his advisers were talented men. A despot gains more advantage from his kingdom if that kingdom is well ruled than otherwise, and difficult though it may be for a despot to override vested interests and to see that the business of the country is done efficiently, it is a task which is not impossible. Sardinia, Piedmont, and Savoy made a country small enough for benevolent despotism to be effective without degenerating into bureaucracy. There always had been a tradition of good government in the country, and it had moreover been under French rule for longer than any other part of Italy. Consequently justice was decently administered, commerce was not hampered by ridiculous imposts, and the orderly state of the countryside made business safe. Sardinia prospered amazingly, in marked contrast to the rest of Italy save Tuscany, and Tuscany was under a Hapsburg who would never risk his chance of the Imperial succession by turning against Austria.

Charles Albert, on the other hand, did his best to display his independence of Austria, and he bestowed a boon of incalculable value upon his people when, between 1830 and 1840, he codified the law of his kingdom. It was not the old Code Napoleon that he re-established—not by any means—but nevertheless it was a good working system of law, here and there perhaps reminiscent of feudalism, here and there obviously influenced by Jesuit thought, but on the whole a vast improvement on the hopeless muddle that had gone before.

Italy—Lombardy, Papal States, Naples, and the Duchies—turned envious and longing eyes on the Kingdom of Sardinia exulting in her prosperity, on her army, forty thousand strong, which guaranteed her (the only sort of guarantee that Austria understood) against Austrian aggression, on her King, who was at least a native of Italy, and on her freedom from the Austrian troops who everywhere else made themselves hideously unpleasant to all and sundry. Opinion was gradually forming that if union could be achieved in no other way annexation by Sardinia would be at least an adequate consolation prize.

Charles Albert at this time offers an interesting character study. He wanted to be the most benevolent of despots at the same time as he hated the idea of being even the least democratic of democrats. He was anxious to give reform to his people in everything save the constitution. Yet at the same time his conscience pricked him, reminding him that at one time he had favoured constitutional reform—that he had even once granted it—and that in his heart of hearts he believed it to be his duty to grant it again, although this generous impulse was over-shadowed by his natural selfishness and ambition. He had sworn to maintain the constitution as it stood, but had he not at one time sworn the exact opposite?

The religious question was a terrible complication. The Pope was definitely against reform, and Charles Albert could hardly oppose his wishes, seeing that he was a sincere Catholic.   All round the King were confessors, Papal nuncios, Jesuits, fanatics, urging him to repression, to condemnation of those who favoured reform, even to the persecution of heresy. He himself was superstitious as well as sincere, and the powers round the throne played subtly on his superstition.   A nun, by name Maria Louisa, appeared, who gained influence over the King and steadfastly opposed all his Liberal aspirations.   She was continually about the palace, counselling, advising, even prophesying when necessary, hysterically playing upon the wretched King's hysterical fears both of this world and the next.   For there was always a chance that he might push his reforms beyond the limit which the Jesuits could tolerate—and even in the enlightened year 1840 such things as poisonings and palace revolutions were not unknown.   Yet assassination was one of the weapons of the wilder section of the republican party.   As the King pitifully explained, he lived between the daggers of the Carbonari and the chocolate of the Jesuits.   Maria Louisa, that remarkable nun, and the officials of the court who were on her side, planned little demonstrations of the evidence of a higher Power's interest in what went on in the Royal Palace.   Mysterious knockings were heard on the walls behind the tapestry ; the spirit of an earlier

Queen of Sardinia—one of the more Catholic ones, of course—was said to have been seen in the corridors watching lest Charles Albert should betray his trust; indeed, matters reached such a pitch that the King even began to hear a mysterious voice when he was alone, telling him what ought to be done. The voice was always on the side of the reactionaries—as was only to be expected when it proceeded, as was later discovered, from a ventriloquial valet in Jesuit pay.

It was surprising that Charles Albert stood the strain. Perhaps the need for continual vigilance and for continual procrastination told on him and left him not at all the man he was. But by the time he had reached the utmost limit of the reforms he was willing to grant all Italy was watching him; the world was waiting for a sign. But the sign did not come from him in the first place. He was too sincere to move without the blessing of the Pope on his enterprise—unless movement were forced on him. As it happened, he gained the blessing of the Pope for long enough for his purpose—or rather, that of the constitutional reformers and Young Italy—and, after that, movement was forced upon him to an extent that made even observers giddy.

CHAPTER III

THE FIRST ATTEMPT

IN the opinion of many, the matter really began with the death of Gregory XVI, in 1846, and the election of Cardinal Mastai-Ferretti as his successor. The new Pope, who assumed the name of Pius IX, had been known for most of his life as one of the few higher dignitaries of the Church who were at all Liberal in their convictions. The moment the result of the election was known—and it came about mainly through a split between the French and Austrian parties arising out of Louis Philippe's intrusion of years ago—a little shudder of expectation ran through Italy, and even spread through Austria and France. There were some who doubted; some who knew how rapidly a Liberal Cardinal becomes a reactionary Pope. Charles Albert of Sardinia had shown how elevation to supreme power alters a man's outlook. But no sooner had Pius ascended the throne of St. Peter than, in the first flush of enthusiasm, he executed an act of clemency which later helped considerably in keeping him Liberal long enough for the business to receive the impetus for which it was waiting. He signed an amnesty to all the political offenders who had suffered under Gregory XVI. The effect was marked. The prisons were cleared of all who entertained Liberal opinions—men who in many cases had been immured and consequently rendered ineffective for years—and it brought all the Italian exiles flocking into the Papal States. Mazzini

28

PIUS IX

left London hurriedly and arrived in Rome, and flung himself into the business of conspiracy with renewed zeal. The combined efforts of all the Liberals led Pius to grant a modified freedom to the press—and prompt use was made of it. The Union of Italy was for the first time openly advocated. But the fact that these first steps had been taken by the least probable of all the Italian potentates—the Pope—led to serious complication. It meant that advocates of union had to make allowance for Pius, and in consequence the suggestion was put forward that he should become head of an Italian confederation—a suggestion which called forth menacing thunder from ever-suspicious Vienna.

It may have been this glittering bait which led Pius a little farther down the slippery path of concession. A Liberalism which would bring him the overlordship of all Italy—the prize which even Cæsar Borgia had failed to grasp—was a Liberalism worth displaying. He began to grant a certain amount of popular representation, and he instituted a Council of State from which laymen were not expressly debarred, and a Civic Guard, destined to be of importance in the later developments.

That was the turning-point in Italian affairs—as far as a continual trend may be said to have a turning-point. Charles Albert in Turin, and his sixteen-year-old son, Victor Emmanuel, were anxiously watching the progress of events. One great reason for the King's opposition to constitutional reform, his deference to the Pope's opinion, now became instead a reason why he should grant it. For the first time for twenty years he allowed himself to speak publicly in favour of reform, and also, with an eye to the rich neighbouring province of Lombardy, he said that he would soon be ready to turn against Austria and liberate Italy.

With each new development the excitement in Italy rose higher than before. Action and reaction played across the countryside like the changing colours of red-hot embers. Soon the blaze was to come. Pius was already rather afraid that he had gone too far, but nothing was more difficult than to draw back. The Austrians would have helped him, of course—they had already occupied, uninvited, one or two of the towns of the turbulent Romagna. But Pius would have nothing to do with the Austrians. Even if the Liberals would not allow him to be master in his own house—and he was not yet really afraid of this happening—he would rather share power with them than hand it over bodily to the Austrians.

Attention was also turned to another step towards union. It was one that might have been insignificant at another time. It had been a mere business arrangement between despots, approved by the reactionary Gregory XVI. Piedmont and Tuscany and the Papal States had entered into a customs union. It was a convenient arrangement. It was economical, it was efficient, and it was inexpensive. Nevertheless, it brought the States into closer contact at a time when close contact was important. Soon after this period, events in Germany showed what effect a customs union had in welding States together. The Italian customs union pointed the way.

Time passed, and the fateful year 1848 was close at hand. Not only Italy, but all Europe was uneasy. There were not wanting signs that a general unheaval was at hand, one more far-reaching even than that of 1830-31. Much of the unrest was undoubtedly due to the example of Italy. The theory that all movements of this sort had their origin in Paris has lately been somewhat discredited. The revolution that converted Louis Philippe, King of the French, into plain Mr. Smith on his way to London, was more probably a result of the Italian troubles than the cause. Very possibly, it was because of reaction to misrule in Italy that the barricades appeared in Paris, that the populace rose in Vienna, that Poles fought Russians to the death on the banks of the Vistula, that the reform movement swelled to ominous dimensions even in placid England, and that the Germans for the first time displayed a tendency to coalesce into a single Empire.

The end of 1847 was marked by the Pope's attempt to give with one hand while he took back with the other. The long-expected constitution was promulgated, and it gave no place in the government save to clerics. That meant that the Pope retained all his power. No cleric, even the most sincerely Liberal, could venture to oppose the Pope, and venal clerics, with an eye to rich preferments, to hats and mitres, were not unknown to Italy. The populace rose in fury against this mockery of a constitution.

Nevertheless, the Pope *had* granted a constitution, and that was all that mattered to Charles Albert. Just when his people's tempers rose to boiling point; just when the demand for reform was verging on a demand for a revolution; just when excitement was generating rebellion, Charles Albert broke his oath to the dead King and issued a constitution.

The deed was done. Twenty-four years ago had Charles Albert sworn that oath, and he had held to it so far. For twenty years he had held unbridled power. Now, at a single gesture, he smirched the honour of the Order of the Annunciation and placed himself in leading strings. Not that it was a very liberal constitution that he granted. He nominated the whole of the Upper House; he retained the irresponsible control of the armed forces of the nation; he could make war and conclude peace as he willed. The first article of the constitution upheld the Roman Faith, and granted bare tolerance to other sects. With an Upper House necessarily of

his party he could be sure that no obnoxious bill
would be passed; with fifty thousand men at his sole
disposal he ought still to be safe against popular
aggression; with peace and war in his hand he could
mould his country's policy as he would. Did he
prove himself capable of wielding the weapons he
still controlled, Charles Albert would find that his
power was as unlimited as ever. But he never had
a chance of proving it.

The Piedmontese were nevertheless overjoyed
at their King's generosity. He bounded into
popularity. There was hardly a disapproving voice
to be heard. Hardly anyone raised a protest at the
flaws in the constitution; hardly anyone darkly
recalled the dreadful days when Charles Albert had
hanged and imprisoned and tortured everyone who
had even mentioned the word " constitution." But
he showed no sign of enjoying his popularity. He
rode through streets of tossing banners, over flowers
cast by cheering multitudes, with a face as pale as
death and a tortured frown knotting his brows. He
was sure he had imperilled—nay, forfeited—his
immortal soul by his violation of his oath. Maria
Louisa, the nun, and his father confessor, assured
him of this and implored him to retract while there
was yet time. And not merely his soul, but the
remnant of his temporal power was in danger, for
the Austrians turned an exceedingly disapproving eye
on his proceedings, and seemed likely to come in
their battalions to set affairs back again in their old
course. That meant either that he would lose his
throne or must consent to rule merely as a crowned
prefect of Austria. The thought of either event was
unbearable.

For the time being no human power could stop
the spread of the Liberal movement in Italy. The
Roman populace obtained a more Liberal Ministry
from the Pope; the Neapolitans obtained a constitution from Ferdinand, while all Sicily rose, clamouring

at one and the same time for autonomy and union with Italy. No one apparently at the time saw the incompatibility of these two demands. Fire and sword did their usual work over the unhappy island, for characteristically, the Neapolitans held by Ferdinand rather than lose their hold on Sicily.

Now came the first movement against the Austrians which gained any measure of success. Young Italy, the remnants of the Carbonari, and all the other secret societies had been working hard in Lombardy and Venice. Their preparations were nearly complete when the great wave of popular feeling forced their hands. Milan rose in revolt.

The Austrian commander-in-chief in Lombardy and Venice at this time was almost the greatest man in Italy. He was Radetsky, a man over eighty years of age, who had held colonel's rank at Marengo nearly fifty years before. As Lombardy revolted, and Venetia rose in sympathy, he found himself cut off from Austria, with an army full of disaffected Italian conscripts, in the midst of a fierce insurgent population. He fought hard. For five days his white-coated regiments, enfeebled by wholesale desertion, struggled to maintain their grasp on Milan. The Tyrolese riflemen picked off rebels in hundreds from the roof of the Duomo. But ammunition ran short, and his men wearied in the ceaseless struggle against the ever-increasing insurgents. At the end of the five days he was forced to conclude an armistice with the Milanese and march his men off in retreat through a furious countryside.

" Councils of War do not fight," said Napoleon. The Milanese Council of War was the exception to the rule. It had fought, and fought hard. It had rejected all Radetsky's proposals for a compromise. When a report arrived that there only remained one day's provisions for the fighting men, they decided

c

that two days' fighting—one unrationed—would clear the city. And two days' fighting did so. Now, with Lombardy in their hands, they proceeded to plan for the future. It would be a very different thing to issue forth and fight Radetsky in the open —raw levies were of vastly less use in the field than in street fighting. An army was wanted at once— an army to strike Radetsky down while he was still reeling from the blow dealt him in Milan. Close at hand there was an army, ready and willing—at the absolute disposal of Charles Albert, King of Sardinia. Already the Unionist movement was strong in Milan, and this last fact settled the matter. Lombardy declared itself united to Sardinia, and sent urgent envoys imploring Charles Albert's help —his immediate help.

Charles Albert thought that then he stood at the parting of the ways. He did not, of course. It was inevitable that he should fight Austria, and it had been ever since he had granted the constitution. But he did not realize it. He still wondered whether he might avoid war, whether Austria would not yield Lombardy tamely to him without a struggle. He hoped that the Great Powers might step in and compose matters. There was no possible chance of this. France was in the throes of her revolution of 1848, and the fact that Venice, which had revolted along with Milan, had declared herself a republic, alienated the other Powers. Republics in those troubled times were vastly distasteful to the Holy Alliance. Yet these and other considerations kept Charles Albert dallying for some precious days, and when at last he took the plunge, declared against Austria, and moved his army, twenty-five thousand strong, into Lombardy, he moved slowly and hesitatingly. He forgot the maxims of his great patron Napoleon—"strike hard, strike quickly."

There was good reason, nevertheless, for this

delay. The army of Sardinia was no more fitted for
war in 1848 than was that of the Second Empire in
1870. There was no staff, no mobilization programme, no transport arrangements, nothing that
makes an army mobile and effective. As soon as
Charles Albert had declared war, and, assuming the
cherished Italian tricolour, sent his divisions streaming forward across the Ticino, everything went to
pieces. The roads were littered with stragglers after
the very first marches. Speed was of the very first
necessity—speed to catch Radetsky, and force him
to battle before he could be reinforced or before he
could rally. But speed is the very quality which half
organized armies are least capable of displaying.
And Charles Albert's army was further handicapped
by the dilatoriness and half-heartedness of its general.
That apt comparison between Charles Albert and
Hamlet is most forcible of all at this time. He was
committed to war—to war to the knife with an
enemy who would be utterly implacable. He had
caught that enemy at a disadvantage, and yet he
failed to profit by it. He delayed, partly through
sheer irresolution, partly because he hoped that the
disadvantages of internal dissension under which the
Austrians laboured would increase (and here he was
misled, for the Hungarians did not take the field
until the next year) and partly because he hoped that
the Austrians, Radetsky in particular, would yield
without a struggle.

But Radetsky was made of sterner stuff. Cut off
from Austria, with destruction staring him in the
face, he yet strove to gather his strength for one last
death grapple, hardly daring to hope that his
preparations would bring him victory as well as
honour. Between Lombardy and Venetia he still had
one refuge, the Quadrilateral. The four fortresses
of Mantua, Peschiera, Legnago and Verona made a
good rallying point. At the moment when the
revolt in Milan took place none of them was in a

good condition for defence, but Radetsky threw himself into the business of equipping them and strengthening them, at the same time stiffening his army in readiness for the blow which he expected at any moment. Could he but hold out for a few months he could expect help, and Radetsky was prepared to do his best, making the most of his four fortresses, maintaining his army in the field to harass the besiegers, and staving off for as prolonged a period as possible what he feared was inevitable.

It was not in the least inevitable. The Sardinian army crawled across Lombardy in the spring of 1848, reached the Mincio, pushed hesitatingly into the Quadrilateral, and then stopped dead for four months. It is amazing when one remembers what Napoleon accomplished in 1796 in this very district. In four months he reduced the Quadrilateral, shattered four Austrian armies, and pushed forward within striking distance of Vienna. Charles Albert was no Napoleon. Reinforcements thronging forward from all over Italy brought the numbers of his army up to over one hundred thousand men, but increase of numbers when all organization was lacking was a disadvantage rather than an advantage. Mantua worried him. He could not devise a plan whereby he could mask that fortress (situated as it was on his best line of communication for an advance) and at the same time keep enough men under his own hand to dispose of Radetsky. It certainly was a troublesome problem—one that had tested Napoleon to the utmost—but Charles Albert made no attempt to solve it.

He turned his attention to Peschiera instead. With Peschiera in his possession he could move more freely into the Quadrilateral. Were he bent on forcing Radetsky to a pitched battle, the capture of Peschiera was his best course. It is greatly to be doubted, however, if he had any mind for such a decisive contest. He was still hoping for a peaceful solution, and perhaps his few tentative movements into the Quadrilateral were merely to satisfy the fire-eaters of his army. Young Victor Emmanuel, at the head of his brigade, and his brother Ferdinand, Duke of Genoa, clamoured for action. Anyone could see that action was imperative, and grew more imperative with every moment that passed. Charles Albert fumbled and boggled and hesitated.

The King was not a good soldier. He had a poor eye for ground, and he was incapable of exact plans of marches and distances, and he had no efficient staff to compensate for this. His divisions were scattered beyond the range of each other's support. From time to time Radetsky came dashing out of the shelter of Verona to beat up the Sardinian lines. Once or twice he met with serious reverses, when by chance he found an Italian division well posted and ready to stand. More usually the Italians were driven from the field, and another blundering combination had to be devised to drive Radetsky back out of harm's way again. The siege of Peschiera progressed languidly.

Then came the news that reinforcements were arriving for Radetsky. Thirty thousand men under Nugent were fighting their way through Venetia to him. The obvious course was for Charles Albert to fling himself on Radetsky and destroy him before Nugent could arrive, but in Charles Albert's present state of mind the obvious was the least likely course. Some Papal troops, without the authority of their government, were on the way to join him. So were some Neapolitans. Charles Albert sent orders for these contingents to cross the Po low down, and, marching round the Quadrilateral, to hold Nugent back. Apparently he did not realize that he was exposing this detachment to almost certain destruction, nor that no operation of this sort would be effective without simultaneous

energetic action against Radetsky. No sooner
did a detachment join Charles Albert than
he tried to find a use for it other than the most
important. He had sent the Tuscan contingent up
past the west side of Lake Garda in an endeavour
to invade Tyrol—a movement from which not the
least benefit could be expected. Anyway, the
Tuscans achieved nothing, for with no transport and
no discipline their marching broke down at once, and
Charles Albert soon hurriedly arrested their snail-
like progress for fear lest Bavaria and the German
Confederation should be offended.

Nugent, the Bayard of the Austrian army, forced
his way steadily through Venetia. His progress was
marked by a succession of battles and sieges. The
Venetian army did not do its utmost to hinder him
—Venetia was a republic, and was not at the disposal
of Charles Albert as were Lombardy and the
Duchies. The curse of division still lay heavy over
Italy. The only opposition Nugent had to meet was
that organized in his immediate path, and this, stout
though it was, was insufficient to hold back thirty
thousand veterans. For the Neapolitan troops never
reached their destination across his route. Ferdinand
of Naples had sent them reluctantly—in fact he had
sent them against his will, forced to do it by popular
opinion. He would rather use his army to slaughter
Sicilians and join Sicily once more to his dominions
before it could join itself to this growing and
dangerous Kingdom of Upper Italy. So he had
bowed to public opinion as little as he might. He
promised fifty thousand men, sent twenty thousand,
delayed their march as much as he could, and as soon
as it was obviously too late for them to interfere
with Nugent he recalled them for use against Sicily.
So in the end Nugent and Radetsky joined hands
at Verona.

As they did so, Peschiera fell. It was the crest
of the wave of Italian success that year—or for ten

years after. Charles Albert was free now to press across the Quadrilateral. He could find no reason left for not flinging himself on Radetsky. But now Radetsky was coming to fling himself on him. The Italian army was weakened by deplorable indiscipline, by abominable commissariat service, and by prolonged inaction. Disease was decimating their ranks, as it always did when men were badly fed and herded together stationary for months. It was even whispered that cholera—the dread enemy which had swept across Italy in 1830—was upon them again. The demoralization of the Italian army had already progressed far enough for the capture of Peschiera to be ineffective in raising its morale.

Radetsky and Nugent came marching up from Verona. Even united their numbers were inferior to Charles Albert's, but there was no question as to which army was superior in effectiveness, nor (or it might be the same thing) as to which was the better led. Charles Albert's seventy thousand were spread over a front of thirty miles. He could neither decide to concentrate and attack, nor to get his dislocated fragments out of harm's way. It was upon these devoted victims that Radetsky flung all the strength and hope of the Austrian Empire.

Radetsky broke the Italian cordon, and bridged and passed the Mincio. Charles Albert hurriedly evacuated the Quadrilateral, abandoning all he had gained, and strove to concentrate and drive the Austrians back. The Italian divisions came pressing up by forced marches—dropping stragglers at every yard—and were flung against the Austrian position at Custozza. Charles Albert's feeble abandonment of the initiative had at last compelled him to a tactical offensive—the half-trained Italian battalions were sent to attack the veteran Austrian units in a strong position strongly entrenched. They very nearly succeeded.

As the guns came flickering into action Charles Albert almost threw off his inertia and despondency. He plunged into the battle, exposing himself all day long, rallying the Italians as they came drifting back, broken, from the Austrian positions. The two princes, Victor Emmanuel and Ferdinand, Duke of Genoa, led their divisions recklessly into action. Custozza was won, and the Austrian position nearly turned, when night fell on the 26th of July. Once more success, decisive and far-reaching, was in the hands of the Italians, but it was snatched away as a result of previous mistakes and mismanagement. To make full use of their partial victory, furious energy and skilful management was necessary. But energy—energy was woefully absent from the Italian higher command. Only a few days before Charles Albert had declined the assistance of Garibaldi, the man who had won twenty actions in South America by his dash and vigour. With Garibaldi in the field now Austria was lost. As it was, the night passed in activity, and the wretched staff organization left the men unfed, the divisions entangled, and the reserves unconcentrated.

Next morning it was the Austrians who attacked. Radetsky had spent the night pulling his army together and massing his reserves at the vital point. Even before the Italian divisions had begun painfully crawling forward to the assault, fifty thousand Austrians crashed into the unready Italian line, dinted it, forced it back, hacked at it and haggled at it. The Tyrolese riflemen harassed the masses of Sardinian infantry, and the fierce Croatian hussars came charging forward at every hint of weakness. The Sardinian reserves arrived slowly and piecemeal, and wasted away as they were sent forward bit by bit. Night fell, and the Italian army still kept together, but the men were unfed, the ammunition was expended, the staff in confusion, and no part of the reserve remained unused to weld the fragments once more together. Retreat, said the panic-stricken staff. Charles Albert prayed to God and consulted his father confessor. The result of this was to confirm him in the belief that retreat was the best course. And retreat meant (so he fondly thought) postponing the issue again for a further space. Charles Albert ordered retreat.

Once, long ago, Napoleon had led a badly-fed army from the Alps past Mantua into Austria. He had won victory after victory. But Napoleon had admitted that his rabble, hard-bitten though it was, would have streamed back to the Alps had it had to retreat a yard before Mantua fell. And Charles Albert's army was a far worse rabble than Napoleon's army of 1796. It had lost twenty-five thousand men at Custozza. It had lost some of its best officers. But worse than all, it had lost heart. As soon as the retreat began it fell to pieces. Whatever discipline it had vanished from the majority of its units.

Radetsky was not the man to slacken pursuit, and to fail to reap full advantage from his hard-won victory. The Austrian divisions swarmed forward, and the Hussars pressed the retreating columns closely and continually. Charles Albert sank back into apathy. There were only two general officers left in the army with any spirit in them, and they were the princes of the royal house. To Victor Emmanuel fell the command of the rearguard. With what remained undisorganized of the army he tried to hold back the triumphant Austrians. Again and again he faced about during that weary march across Lombardy, and beat back the enemy as they pressed the pursuit too hard. But nothing could save that motley horde. Desertion and disease thinned the ranks and reduced the army to a dwindling mass of fugitives. They tried to make a stand before Milan, but it was useless. All that Charles Albert could do for his friends was to enter

into a military convention whereby the town was
spared from assault and sack. The negotiations led
to an armistice, which Radetsky was strangely
willing to grant. In exchange for an unimpeded
retreat to Piedmont, and some months' peace
when he arrived there, Charles Albert abandoned
Lombardy, Venice, and the Duchies to the
Austrians.

The reasons why Radetsky was willing to grant
the armistice were many and diverse. His army had
been hard hit at Custozza. There was no doubt
about that. Then his communications were still
insecure. Lombardy in his rear was still in revolt;
so was Venice. He wanted time to consolidate his
position. But the military reasons were the least
important—security of communications and solidity
of position had not been essential to a man like
Radetsky during the fateful months of 1848. But
the political situation was more involved still.
England had regarded the beginnings of the Italian
rising with a nearly approving eye—she did not like
the Republicans, but demands for constitutions and
parliamentary government appealed to her sympathy,
and flattered her pride. And she was genuinely
shocked by the accounts of the horrible deeds of
Austrian troops and despotic police throughout the
peninsula. She had offered her mediation once
before, when Charles Albert was about to enter the
Quadrilateral, but then the King, at the height of
his good fortune, had rejected the offer. " *Italia
farà da se,*" said Charles Albert.

Yet England was repeating her offer now.
France, too, was regarding the struggle in Italy with
an interested eye. She was anxious to secure Savoy
and Nice, and in exchange for the cession of this
territory she would intervene on Sardinia's behalf.
Charles Albert and his ministry had haughtily
declined the offer, but now Radetsky feared that
they might yield if driven to extremity. Were

peace negotiations to open, Piedmont's retention of the Duchies might be a serious factor. It was worth abandoning considerable military advantage to make sure of the possession of Parma and Modena—especially as the memory of this abandonment might easily rankle in the future. So Radetsky granted Charles Albert's plea for an armistice, and Lombardy, Venice, Parma and Modena were handed over to the tender mercies of the Austrians.

The news of the defeat at Custozza and the armistice that followed sent a shudder through Italy. It encouraged the reactionaries, and at the same time it drove the violent Liberals to frenzy. Excited followers of Mazzini told of Charles Albert's last journey through Milan; how the populace shouted to him that he had betrayed them; how they menaced him and hustled him until he had to call on his soldiers to protect him; they omitted reference to the fact that Charles Albert, goaded by the taunts of the mob, had offered to turn back and continue the hopeless struggle under the walls of the town; but they declared, almost triumphantly, that the hated King had once more deserted his friends and betrayed his trust. Consequently, they said, the only hope of Italy lay in a republic. The flames of republicanism leaped higher than before—until they were drowned in floods of blood on the inevitable arrival of the Austrians.

In Parma and Modena the rulers came back under Austrian protection : that was the state of affairs prevailing before the revolt. In Tuscany, Leopold, too, was forced to call for the same assistance, although before the war he had always indignantly refused to tolerate Austrian interference. It was the action of the extremists that compelled him to it. One satisfactory eventual result it had, nevertheless. It discredited the Mazzinists, and the unbearable rule of the Austrian army exasperated the people not merely with the Austrians, but with the dynasty, erstwhile fairly popular, and thus removed one difficult stumbling block from the path to unity.

In the Papal States the popular clamour soon out-Heroded Herod—soon became more Liberal than Pius—and the Pope, finding his power slipping away from him at the same time as his popularity, his army disobeying orders and proceeding to fight nations with whom he was supposed to be in a state of peace, and further reforms demanded of him with hardly-veiled threats, eventually gave up the struggle, and discredited himself for ever with the Italian party by flying from the country and taking refuge in Ferdinand of Naples' fortress of Gaeta. His departure made room for the Republicans—Mazzini and the rest—who proceeded, regardless of the impending menace of an Austrian invasion, with the erection of a Roman Republic, adorned with Triumvirs and the rest, and utterly careless about the fate of the cause of liberty in the rest of the country.

Disruptive tendencies were noticeable elsewhere. Sicily tried to break free from Naples, even going as far as to offer the crown of Sicily to the Duke of Genoa, Victor Emmanuel's brother. The offer was declined, for Charles Albert had to keep on good terms with the King of Naples; besides, he was aiming at the union of Italy, not at its further partition. In time, Ferdinand, having recalled his troops from the fighting in Lombardy, was able to shatter the separatist party, and to conquer the island without even the assistance of Austria. The bombardment of Messina earned him the name of King Bomba; his unspeakable cruelties everywhere saw to it that the island remained tranquil; but he ruined himself in the eyes of England, and the unstable military despotism that he built up was bound to collapse as soon as the fancy of the army was taken by a greater man than he.

The armistice between Austria and the Kingdom of Sardinia was concluded on August 5th, 1848. Then Charles Albert came home, to render, for the first time, an account to the government he had erected. He was still popular, and the hard fighting of his sons had done much to remove the stain of military failure from the dynasty. So he was received gravely but kindly. The deputies in Turin made endless speeches—it must be remembered that they had not enjoyed the privilege of free speech very long—and a select committee made elaborate investigations into the reasons for the defeat. They published a long report, in which they declared that the disastrous result was due to bad staff work, to bad discipline, to hesitation on the part of the higher command; but they found a salve for the national *amour propre* by hinting that treason must have played a part as well. It was a very fine report indeed, from a parliamentary point of view, or even from a rhetorical one; the only objections to it were that in places it was incorrect, it was nowhere constructive and everywhere critical, and it told no one anything that he did not know already.

The speeches and reports flowed smoothly on. Charles Albert was plunged into a slough of diplomacy from which a better man than he would have found it hard to emerge with success. England, Germany, Russia, France, all dallied with the idea of interference or of putting pressure on Austria, but they all dropped away, while Austria put down the rebellion that had almost torn her to pieces, built up her army, secured her hold on Lombardy and Venetia (with the exception of Venice itself) and prepared to fight if she were not granted all her demands, which rose steadily as her position grew more secure, until at last the *status quo* was the least that would satisfy her. On the one side there was energetic military preparation. On the other there were speeches, reports, uninspired diplomacy;

of military preparation or reform on the part of
Sardinia there was absolutely nothing, unless the
huddling together of recruits in new regiments
without attempting to train and equip them can be
termed preparation.

No attempt was made to organize a transport
train, or to devise a staff system that would work
even fairly satisfactorily. The gunners hardly knew
how to load their guns; the infantry in large part
actually remained in ignorance of how to use the
percussion cap muskets with which most of them were
armed. There was only one thing that Charles
Albert did, and that he did badly. He found a
general. He determined to have his army
commanded by a man who had not been in Italy
more than a few weeks; who could not speak a word
of Italian; who was unknown to the rank and file and
hated by the generals; whose military training had
been brief, whose experience in command in the field
was nil, whose capacity was hardly greater than his
own, and whose name could never arouse enthusiasm
in that it was utterly unpronounceable.

The reasons which impelled Charles Albert to this
extraordinary appointment of Chrzanowsky to the
command-in-chief of the Sardinian army were
characteristic. One may confidently deduce that
Maria Louisa, the nun, and the father confessors,
had been at work. Charles Albert thought that
Chrzanowsky was filled with a certainty of divine
inspiration in his task.

It is strange that the King, with the strong
vein of superstition that ran through his character,
never stopped to think of the career of that other
Charles Albert in history, which so curiously
resembled his. Doctor Johnson has some lines about
him in "The Vanity of Human Wishes." He was
a "bold Bavarian" who tried to wrest the Imperial
dignity from the Hapsburgs at the time of Maria
Theresa. He was successful for a brief while, but

then, deserted and defeated, he crept away to die
" from anguish and from shame." The Sardinian
Charles Albert might have been expected to take
warning from this, but curiously he did not. He
was not consistent even in his superstition.

The armistice dragged on and on, and it became
vital that Charles Albert should do something
decisive. Diplomacy and the pleas of the Powers had
won nothing for him. He had to choose between
staying contented with what he had or making
another effort at conquest. If he made peace, he
was awkwardly situated. The Custozza campaign
had been too much a fiasco and not great enough
a disaster, and a monarch is more susceptible to
ridicule than to hatred. Charles Albert could not
bear the thought of all his people jeering at him, at
the high hopes he had entertained when he set out
for Milan, at his projected " Kingdom of Upper
Italy." He had done either too much or not
enough. Nothing could be undone; therefore
Charles Albert had to do more. He denounced the
armistice, and led the forces of Piedmont (under their
unpronounceable general) against the army of the
Austrian Empire. He was setting himself enough
to do now.

Over one hundred thousand men poured forward across the Sesia. Chrzanowsky (imagine the
Bersaglieri charging forward shouting " Viva
Chrzanowsky ! ") devised the usual second-rate plan
of the usual second-rate general. Milan was his
objective. He thrust forward for Milan with his left,
leaving a couple of divisions out on his right, which
was peculiarly liable to attack on account of the
widely diverging lines of communication open to the
Austrians in their position behind the Ticino with
Milan almost on their extreme right.

Radetsky acted with energy and vigour, if not
with brilliance. He concentrated on his left,
guarding his communications through Cremona and

Mantua, and then passed the Ticino from Pavia upward. Ramorino was the Sardinian general in command of the divisions in the neighbourhood. He had a golden opportunity. It is easy to imagine what would have happened had Napoleon and Davout been in the places of Chrzanowsky and Ramorino. The Austrian advance would have been held up; the other Sardinian divisions would have come swarming down from the Milan-Vercelli road; there would have been a brief, fierce struggle. Then the massed guns would have broken the Austrian resistance. A wild attack (Ney would have headed it) would have flung the Austrians back routed, with the Po and the Ticino across their rear. Hemmed into the angle between the rivers there could only have been disaster for the Austrians. It would have been another Friedland—and what sort of Tilsit would have followed?

But Ramorino was no Davout. He flinched from the collision, and not merely avoided the Austrian advance, but took his men right across the Po, away from the approaching battle. It would not even have been so bad had he retreated before the Austrians. His division would still have been of use. As it was, his twenty thousand men might not have been recruited for all the good they were to the army.

The ticklish moment past, Radetsky swung his columns round to the right and rushed upon the enemy. The Sardinians, thanks to their frightful disorganization and indiscipline, had so far only succeeded in marching one-third of the distance the Austrians had covered. No power on earth could concentrate them in time to move towards the Austrians. The staff bustled wildly and ineffectively. The leading columns were turned back, the rearmost ones bidden to hasten—with resulting dislocation of the supply system. Yet the scattered divisions could not be brought out of harm's way. Radetsky pushed forward relentlessly, tumbling one division after another into ruin as he came across them. He found the bulk of the Sardinian army in position at last at Novara.

Thanks to their concentration on their left, and to their unwieldiness in manœuvre, the Sardinians found themselves forced to form front to a flank, with their sole line of communication running immediately behind their line. Victory or destruction—there was no third possibility—lay before them. To a disciplined army it might have been stimulating. To the Sardinians it was very much the reverse.

On the morning of the battle, Charles Albert rode out on his black horse, wrapped in a black and silver cloak. The troops raised a feeble cheer, but the King hardly noticed it. He was worried and flurried. It is difficult to find any reference to Chrzanowsky. His activities were not obvious.

The Austrians attacked the Sardinian left, at Bicocca. At first they were successful, but Victor Emmanuel brought up his Savoyards and retook the position. An even struggle developed here. Then the Austrians flung themselves on the Sardinian centre at Citadella. The place was taken and retaken repeatedly. All along the line the Tyrolese riflemen picked off the officers at long range; the Austrian guns cut lanes through the massed Sardinian squares in their exposed position. The strain on the wretched undisciplined troops was terrible, yet they held on, fighting desperately whenever they could come to grips with their opponents. But Chrzanowsky could not make use of their wild valour. When Victor Emmanuel and Ferdinand, Duke of Genoa, led forward the twenty-first of the line and stormed Citadella the whole Austrian line reeled. Chrzanowsky might have flung in his reserves and saved the day, but he was slow, the troops themselves were unhandy, and the golden opportunity

D

was lost. Radetsky pulled his men together, and attacked more fiercely than before. As the strain grew more intense he massed his forces on his right. Chrzanowsky had frittered away all his reserves, and could not ward off the blow. Twenty thousand men stormed Bicocca, though Victor Emmanuel, with reckless bravery, strove to hold them back. The Sardinians hesitated, and then broke, all along the line. The fate of Italy was for the time decided.

Charles Albert, black cloak flying, came riding through the wreck, seeking the death which Fate denied him. " All is lost, even honour," he wailed pitifully to Chrzanowsky. His staff, with mistaken kindness, caught his bridle and forced him from the field. The Sardinian army, with its glimmering of military education, realizing what it meant as they were thrust back beyond their only road home, dissolved away into disconnected fragments, and when night fell half the army had deserted and was streaming by by-roads back to Piedmont. There was not even a rearguard left this time for Victor Emmanuel to lead against the enemy.

That night, as was inevitable, Sardinian envoys rode into Radetsky's lines to plead for an armistice. The terms were harsh—Radetsky could exact what he liked, seeing that the Sardinian army was in his power. The Lombard volunteers must be disbanded; the army must retreat at once to the Ticino; all Piedmont between the Sesia and the Ticino must be delivered over to the Austrians, and the fortress of Alessandria as well; and Victor Emmanuel must be handed over as a hostage.

Charles Albert could not bring himself to drain the bitter cup which his presumption and carelessness had brought him. He could not set his name to a document in which he confessed this new failure. He feared lest the terms were so rigorous because of Austrian dislike for him personally. He announced to his assembled staff that he abdicated, and rode straightway from that camp of misery, away from his army, away from his country, to hide his shame in a Portuguese monastery. He only survived his ruin for three months. The mantle of his disaster descended upon the shoulders of young Victor Emmanuel, aged twenty-nine.

CHAPTER IV

RECOVERY

IT was a strange moment for an accession, and it might have been thought ominous by anyone not so matter-of-fact as Victor Emmanuel.

At nine o'clock on that spring evening, with a beaten army round him, a victorious enemy between him and his capital, his men deserting by hundreds every hour as the night passed, Victor Emmanuel became King of Sardinia. He received the homage of his court by the light of the camp-fire, and then set out to obtain what terms he could from the implacable Radetsky.

His father's abdication had no effect in easing the armistice terms offered, save that he was saved the humiliation of having to give hostages. It is just possible that Radetsky thought him more likely to keep his word than his father—or less dangerous. But that was the only lightening of the burden. The army still had to retire behind the Sesia, still had to hand over Alessandria, still had to place Sardinia at the mercy of the Austrians. The army trailed back miserably to Turin, beaten in a week's campaign by less than their own numbers, and not merely beaten, but utterly routed. As Charles Albert had said, all was lost, including honour. The people received both King and army with icy coldness.

On his arrival Victor Emmanuel published a proclamation. In it he made an announcement that was to exercise a permanent influence over the history of Italy. He declared that he was going to

throw himself heart and soul into the business of
building the army afresh, of consolidating the constitution, and of maintaining liberty in Sardinia even
if it was expelled from the rest of the peninsula, and
he begged his people to give him all the help that
lay in their power.

At first this seemed hardly likely. The parliament refused to recognize the inevitable and
clamoured for a continuation of the war; they
declared that the minister who handed over
Alessandria to the Austrians would be guilty of
treason; they found fault with every single one of
the terms of the armistice. It was a bad start for
the new reign.

As though this was not enough for the King to
bear, Mazzini and the Republicans started fresh
trouble. Mazzini stung the people of Genoa, his
native town, to revolt, demanding the separation of
Genoa from Sardinia and its recognition as a
republic. In themselves these demands display
Mazzini's lack of political insight and his utter recklessness of the consequences that might ensue for
his friends. Even were Sardinia to tolerate the loss
of Genoa, which was hardly likely, it was certain
that Austria, flushed with her victories of Custozza
and Novara, would not allow for a moment the
existence in Italy of an independent republic. If
Austrian were substituted for Sardinian rule the
Genoese would find themselves under King Stork.
Nevertheless, urged on by Mazzini, the Genoese rose
and took possession of the place. In the neighbourhood was Ramorino, the man who had failed Charles
Albert before Novara, with a division of Italian
troops. Ramorino was an old Carbonaro and
republican, and the new republic built high hopes on
his assistance, but he hesitated just as he had done
when Radetsky crossed the Ticino. The rebellion
was the first circumstance which arose to bind the
new King to his people. The national vanity had

already been sufficiently mortified by the recent events. No one in Piedmont would hear of the separation of Genoa. Confident in the goodwill of his people, Victor Emmanuel sent his army to put the rebellion down. La Marmora, senior general of division, was in command. He marched for the town with a rapidity unusual in Piedmontese armies, reached the outskirts before he was expected and long before the talkative Mazzinists had made any preparations for defence, and then, in two successive assaults, captured first the forts and then the town. The Sardinians pillaged a little, ravished a little, murdered a little, but on the whole exhibited remarkable self-restraint. The movement ended in very little bad blood between Genoa and the rest of the country.

The great point was the Sardinian army had shown that they were of some use in war after all, and it taught the few who were desirous of displacing the dynasty that their hopes were vain. National *amour propre* was salved, and when Victor Emmanuel, with a first stroke of dexterous parliamentarianism, dissolved the Chamber the elections that followed (there is some hint, however, that they were " managed ") gave him a large majority which acquiesced in the terms of the armistice. It was the only sensible thing to do.

The peace terms that followed were not unbearable. For this Victor Emmanuel was alone to be thanked. He combined bluster with firmness and with occasional diplomatic hints that perhaps he would not be as unwilling as was his father to call in French assistance. That threat saved the day. The last thing the Austrians wanted was to see the French given an opportunity of poaching on their own special preserve of Italy. In the end Sardinia had to cede no territory, and had only to submit to an Austrian occupation of a limited area while the war indemnity—three millions sterling—was being paid. The precious constitution was saved. The Austrians were profuse in their hints that the war indemnity would not be demanded if the constitution were suppressed, and they of course assured Victor Emmanuel that he could count on their help against his subjects should they object to the suppression.

But Victor Emmanuel was made of stout stuff. He was not going to reign only by the grace of Austria. If he could not be King of Sardinia by the free will of his subjects he would not be King at all, and he had no objection to being a constitutional King if that were demanded of him. Theoretically, Victor Emmanuel was a good constitutionalist, and if in practice his sturdy independence fretted against the bonds, he was soon to find that they were not very galling, especially since there was to arise in the Sardinian Parliament a man distinguished as the foremost parliamentarian of his age, who showed that it was easier for a man to control a country constitutionally even than by the machinery of despotism.

The peace negotiations finished, and Genoa pacified, Victor Emmanuel at last had time to look round him and form a true estimate of his position. It was far sounder than it had been at the start. The subjection of Genoa had helped. So had his stout championship of the constitution. One more step was needed to save the national self-respect and to whitewash a little the memory of Charles Albert. General Ramorino was a dangerous man. He had equivocated during the Genoese troubles, and he was strongly suspected of disaffection. Ramorino was arrested, put on his trial for his disobedience to orders at the opening of the Novara campaign and promptly shot. He deserved it without a doubt. But nevertheless there is no avoiding the fact that by shooting Ramorino Victor Emmanuel was killing two, or even three, birds with one stone. He was finding a scapegoat for the recent disaster; he was showing

that Charles Albert might have been successful had
he had capable subordinates, and he was getting rid
of a turbulent and dangerous conspirator.

Now, the shame of the recent peace being a
little forgotten, the Sardinians were better able to
appreciate their great good-fortune as compared with
the citizens of the other states of Italy. Naples and
Sicily were in a frightful condition—a worse condition
than they had ever been in before, which is saying
a great deal. Torture and executions and semi-legal
murder were common happenings there. Corruption
throughout the whole country; civil war always a
menacing possibility; crushing taxation; a ruling
dynasty abominably cruel and dissolute; and over all
the menace of Austria, were what the people of the
Two Sicilies had to endure. In the Papal States
French and Austrian soldiers had put down Mazzini's
republic, and Pius had come back from Gaeta a
confirmed reactionary, with all the intolerance and
cruelty of a renegade. Rome had fallen before the
assaults of Oudinot's infantry, and Garibaldi had
fled across Italy pursued by the soldiers of three
nations. Men told with bated breath of how his
lovely wife, far advanced in pregnancy, had refused
to leave him, and had accompanied him on his wild
march. How a mad Englishman, once a colonel in
the Guards, had commanded the rearguard, dressed
in the tail-coat and tall hat that convention demanded
of retired colonels. How Garibaldi had seen his
beloved Anita die through lack of medical attention
near Ravenna, without a woman within call. They
told the horrible story of how Garibaldi later, hidden
in an inner room in an inn, had heard peasants
discussing among themselves the fact that dogs had
dragged out Anita's body from the shallow grave he
had dug, and had devoured it to the bones.

Garibaldi had escaped, luckily for Italy. His
followers were shot and hanged and racked and
quartered all over Italy. In Tuscany the Grand

Duke now reigned with the assistance of an Austrian garrison, and his kindly personal rule was exchanged for martial law administered by an alien soldiery. In Modena the abominable Francis had been once more empowered to work his will on his hapless subjects.

The fate of Lombardy and Venice—the country that the Sardinians had marched to free—was worse than all. The late rebels were executed in hundreds. Some cities still held out. Brescia was the foremost. Radetsky sent Nugent against the town with thirty thousand men. Nugent, the most chivalrous of men, fell in the assault, and was succeeded by the unspeakable Haynau even as the city fell into his hands. Brescia was sacked from end to end. No prisoners were taken : almost every man in the place was slain. The women were more unfortunate. Every house in the whole two provinces in which arms were found was burned. Executions wiped out what was left of the rebels. Then, the provinces pacified, the Austrians restored the normal rule of espionage, torture, the flogging of women in the streets, and the imprisonment without trial of suspects.

When the Austrians found that the Italians of Milan and Venice refrained from going to the theatre because Austrians were to be seen there, they published a notice stating that everyone who did not go to the theatre would be suspect, and therefore liable to arbitrary imprisonment, torture to exact confession, and death. Agents provocateurs egged on the people to silly conspiracies and demonstrations, each succeeded by the usual crop of floggings and hangings. Mazzini did the same, with a like result. The situation of Lombards and Venetians was too awful for description.

With these examples before them the Sardinians realized that they were lucky in their dynasty. Victor Emmanuel rose in the popular estimation for

his refusal to tolerate Austrian interference. To
analyse the situation down to its elements, it was a
choice between the House of Savoy and the rule
of Austria; no third course was open to them. No
one, not even the most hot-headed republican, could
hesitate for a moment in his choice. So Victor
Emmanuel found himself firmly established as soon
as the excitement over Novara was over, and he
soon set out to add personal popularity as another
reason for the permanence of the dynasty.

In the army he was already popular. Everyone
remembered his reckless courage at Custozza and
Novara and half a dozen other actions. He was a
soldier through and through, and the rank and file
loved him for the reforms that he brought about for
their benefit. The officers, still largely drawn from
the class of the one-time feudal nobility, were stimulated by his courteous attitude towards them. And in
La Marmora, the captor of Genoa, he found a man
who, while anything but a good general, was at least
an extremely efficient clerk—the ideal War Minister
under a King who knew what was needful and was
able to ensure that it was done.

Among the people, especially among the
Piedmontese peasantry, there was already a certain
vague respect for the kingly dignity dating back
from feudal times. In the towns it was rather
different, but the King's popularity increased
steadily as folk found that he was a man of his
word, determined on the efficient government of his
people, and strong-willed enough to carry through
any project he conceived that would help towards
that end.

Parliament was different. The deputies were
still drunk with free speech, and were prone to
criticize everything that came within range, and to
talk instead of act at every possible moment. The
" Block " system, the curse of nearly every Continental Parliament, left every ministry dependent

upon the goodwill of the leaders of half a dozen different little parties, with the not unnatural result that the life of each successive government was fleeting. The King was plagued with the inability to get any work done at all. The ratification of the treaty with Austria was delayed, until at last he was forced to issue a proclamation (the " Proclama di Moncalien ") in which it was broadly hinted that if Parliament did not hurry on with the matter Victor Emmanuel would have to find some other means of managing the business of State. That was effective, and the new parliament which was summoned accepted the treaty.

Its next step was one which had been over-delayed. It abolished the fantastic rights of the church. A series of laws deprived the Jesuits of their control over education, the clergy as a body of its right of trial by its own courts, and ecclesiastical edifices in general of the right of sanctuary. There was some murmuring among the priest-ridden people at this rather arbitrary act, but the short-sighted clericals cut the ground from under their own feet by an act of extraordinary intolerance and still more extraordinary short-sightedness. Santa Rosa, the minister mainly responsible, fell ill immediately afterwards, and, at the point of death, asked for the Sacrament. It was refused him, and Santa Rosa died without the viaticum. The whole trend of public opinion turned against the priesthood in consequence of this, and Santa Rosa's funeral was attended by huge crowds of sympathizers from all over Piedmont.

The stars in their courses fought for Victor Emmanuel at this juncture. The circumstances attending Santa Rosa's death had neutralized the opposition to him of the most powerful of the Conservative class, and the mad rebellion of Genoa had shown the recklessness and folly of the extreme Liberals. And, what was more important than

either, Santa Rosa's death made room in the Cabinet
for the greatest politician in Europe, Camillo Cavour.

Cavour so far had done little creative work. He
had held a commission in the army, which was only
natural, seeing that his father was a marquis of the
old nobility, but he had got into trouble as a Liberal
during Charles Albert's early repressive régime, and
had left the army and had studied farming. At the
same time, nevertheless, he had continued to dabble
in politics, combining, in the usual Continental way,
politics and journalism. The *Risorgimento*, the
paper he started in Turin in 1847, had expressed
vigorous but moderate Liberal views, and Cavour
had entered Parliament similarly as a moderate
Conservative. His friends claimed for him that he
had been the first to express the need for a constitution, and that an article by him had been the spur
which had sent Charles Albert marching into
Lombardy in 1848, but these claims are too far-
reaching ever to be granted. All that may be said
is that Cavour certainly had early shown sympathy
with the popular voice and a fearless expression of it.
His speeches on the anti-clerical legislation had first
brought him into general notice, and it was Victor
Emmanuel who was earliest aware of his vast ability.

So Cavour joined the Cabinet, first as Minister
of Agriculture and later as Minister of Finance,
serving under the talented, cultured, honest Massimo
d'Azeglio, who by now was gravely overstrained, and
who was becoming a little too timid with advancing
years.

The King was aware that Cavour was the man
for his purpose, and Cavour was aware that the King
was a man to be relied on. Consequently the trust
and confidence between these two developed wonder-
fully, and Victor Emmanuel's not inconsiderable
influence could be relied on always to support the
Minister whom he knew was indispensable to the
cause of Sardinia and Italy. Before Cavour, how-

ever, could attain full power, a good deal of
manœuvring had to take place in the Piedmontese
Parliament. D'Azeglio was not the man to give way
to his subordinate quietly, and, thanks to the consistent support of Conservatives of all shades of
opinion, he held a position from which he could not
be ousted at once. And to Cavour many of the
Conservatives were of no use at all. Even if he were
to succeed d'Azeglio as Prime Minister and hold
office by virtue of a Conservative majority, that very
fact would seriously restrict the courses of action
open to him. Moderate Liberalism was his need,
and a few deft moves on the political chessboard
enabled him to satisfy it. A few telling speeches
gained him a following in the House, and Cavour
was able to split both the Liberal and the Conservative parties and attach to himself those sections of
them which were of use to them. The reactionary
Conservatives and the Republican Liberals were alike
excluded, and, forming the Opposition as they did,
they were divided and hopeless against Cavour's
triumphant coalition, to say nothing of the fact that
the influence of the King over the Conservatives,
which was great, hindered them from opposing
Cavour with any degree of animosity.

It was not accomplished in a moment, of course.
For a space d'Azeglio more than held his own, and
Cavour once found it advisable to leave Piedmont
and go for a tour round Europe, but he triumphed
in the end, and took office in 1852 with an overwhelming majority as President of the Council and
Minister of Finance. Then he and Victor Emmanuel
were in a position to look round and plan the opening
moves of the new campaign for Italian unity.

CHAPTER V

THE SEARCH FOR AN ALLY

OF the first importance was the need to make the kingdom strong enough to have a large say in the affairs of the world. At present it was still weak and seriously open to attack. The finances were very involved, thanks to the need to pay the indemnity to Austria. Various loans called for as much as eight per cent. interest. Cavour took the matter in hand, and at the end of a year, thanks to his financial ability, the indemnity to Austria was paid off and the country cleared of the Austrians, while the credit of the kingdom was so much improved that it was possible to take some steps towards the funding of the debt and the reduction of the rate of interest.

The resources of the country needed developing. The most obvious deficiency was in communications. Cavour threw himself into the business. He raised money somehow—part of it came from a sequestration of the property of religious houses—and built roads and railways wherever he could. The building of the line between Turin and Genoa was followed by a vast increase in the trade of the country. At the end of the year, so obvious was the improvement that he was emboldened to launch himself once more on the troublous sea of a general election, which established him with a greater majority than ever, so that he could push through all urgent reforms with the least possible delay.

It was Cavour who first suggested the tunnel

CHARLES ALBERT
KING OF SARDINIA

under Mont Cenis, and was laughed at for his pains by half the engineers of Europe. It was Cavour who raised, partly by public subscription throughout Italy, the funds to fortify the frontier and make the country fairly safe in case of a surprise attack by Austria. By a vigorous free trade policy he was able to help along the established industries of the country, and this development brought Sardinia into friendly contact with England and France.

The Sardinian Liberals were pleased with anti-clerical measures, such as that introducing and making compulsory civil marriage, and another which abolished the mendicant orders; the Conservatives were pleased with the reform of the army and the organization of the national defences. All classes shared in the prosperity which peace and energetic government brought them.

The change in the condition of the country in two years was simply astonishing. Victor Emmanuel was now head of a State united, strong, enthusiastic, even wealthy, comparatively speaking, with a constitutional government more stable than the old despotism had ever been, an army that could be relied on, and a fleet that could over-match anything that Italy or Austria could show. Clearly something could now be done in the matter which lay nearest to his heart.

Of one thing Victor Emmanuel was convinced. He based all his policy upon this conviction. That was that Italy could never free herself from Austria without assistance. Charles Albert, his father, had never admitted such a thing for a moment. "*Italia farà da se*," said Charles Albert, and he lost his throne endeavouring to prove himself right. Victor Emmanuel thought he was wrong, and a good many people have come to the same conclusion. But it is just possible that he was right. It hardly seems likely that Austria would have retained her grip on Italy in the face of steady Sardinian opposition for

very long. Sooner or later there would arise another
favourable opportunity for Sardinian intervention in
Lombardy or elsewhere, and another Custozza might
be fought with a different result.   The benefit to
the dynasty and to Italy would be immense if Italy
were to combine as a result of her own exertions
directed by the House of Savoy.   It would be an
achievement to be remembered for all time; it would
give the new nation a ready-made history that would
be something to be proud of.

Yet, at the time at least, Victor Emmanuel and
Cavour—two of the keenest minds of the age—did
not think it was possible.   The King's views may
have changed a little, later (as witness the occasion
when he said that Italy was made too easily), but
at present he had decided definitely that the first
step towards the unification of Italy was to find an
ally who would help Sardinia against Austria.

It was not going to be easy.   England was
sympathetic, but was unlikely to plunge into a
Continental war merely that Lombardy and Venetia
might be added to Victor Emmanuel's dominions—
not even though Victor Emmanuel had some claim
to consideration as the rightful King of England.[1]
Parliamentary institutions and eight hundred years
of Royal descent might make England look with a
favourable eye on Sardinia, but it would need some
substantial inducement to cause England to give
more than her countenance to the movement.   Only
a gift as valuable as, say, Malta would be of any
avail; certainly Nelson had once recommended to
his government the acquisition of Sardinia, but
Victor Emmanuel would not hear of giving up
Sardinia.

At the time, no other country had any friendly
feeling for Sardinia.   Napoleon III had climbed to

---

[1] Through Henrietta, daughter of Charles I. She married the
Duke of Orleans, and her daughter married Victor Amadeus I,
through whose daughter the claim was transmitted to the line of
Carignano.

the throne of France, but the recent anti-clerical
legislation had annoyed him, and he was too busy
just at the moment establishing himself firmly on
his rickety throne to bother about small nations.
Compared to the enmity of Russia, the friendship
of Piedmont was but a small thing.

There was no hope at all from Prussia or Russia.
The rulers of those countries had lately been seriously
remonstrating with Victor Emmanuel for his refusal
to repeal his constitutional reforms. They would be
far more likely to help in wiping the Kingdom of
Piedmont off the map than to assist in extending
its sway.

These were all difficulties, but they were not the
most important. The greatest difficulty was that the
Powers refused to take the Kingdom of Sardinia
seriously. They remembered the hesitation and the
changeful policy of Charles Albert, and they remembered how twice his army had been utterly routed
by the Austrians. They could not believe that any
good could come out of a State that had failed so
lamentably and repeatedly. Sardinia could hardly
claim pre-eminence in Italy on the strength of her
two defeats. Ferdinand of Naples, strictly speaking,
had been more successful. He had put down his
rebels and had reunited his kingdom unaided.
There was a desperate need for Sardinia to do
something to show that she was a factor to be considered, something to prove that she had a right to
call the attention of the Powers to her needs and
ambitions. Victor Emmanuel and Cavour went on
building up their finances, their army, and their
fleet, patiently waiting for an opportunity to use
them. It came soon enough.

There were several reasons why Napoleon III
wanted to go to war with Russia. In the first place
the Tsar, alone among the monarchs of Europe, had
refused to recognize him as Emperor when news of
the proclamation came through; he alone had

E

declined to call Napoleon " *mon frère.*" Then
besides, Napoleon had to " embark on a spirited
foreign policy " to keep his people interested. If
he had to fight someone, he would rather it were
Russia than anyone else, for, save for England (and
he had too much sense to fight *her*), Russia had done
more than any other country in the pulling down of
his Imperial uncle. Lastly, he was in need of the
alliance of England, and the only country that
England might be induced to fight was, similarly,
Russia.   England   strongly   suspected   Russia   of
designs upon Constantinople, and, in accordance with
her traditional policy, she would fight rather than see
that city and the Dardanelles in the possession of
the Tsar.

So when it came about that Russia thought
herself strong enough to brave the Powers and put
forward claims as protector of the Christians in the
Sultan's dominions, Napoleon did not find much
difficulty in inducing England to come to the support
of Turkey, and the disagreement developed into war.
In the beginning of 1854 the allied French and
English landed in Turkey, found that the Turks
could maintain their Danubian frontier unaided, and
so proceeded to transfer to the Crimea, to carry the
war to the place most in dispute, where Russia was
building up a great Black Sea base.

Napoleon had not succeeded in carrying any
other Power with him into the struggle.   Austria
had obstinately remained neutral—she could hardly
do otherwise, seeing that she was indebted to Russia
for the reconquest of Hungary five years before—
while Germany in general was more inclined to the
Russian side than to the French.

However, the allied armies, forty thousand strong
and more, began their venture successfully.   They
landed, cleared a path to Sebastopol by their victory
at the Alma, and settled down (after considerable
delay, which permitted the reorganization of the

defences) to besiege the fortress. They beat off two great efforts by the Russians at Inkermann and Balaclava, but although those armies, fresh from forty years of peace, could fight, they could do little else. Five miles only of road constituted their line of communication, bad road, admittedly, but the arrangement of supplies utterly broke down. Bad staff work at home, bad staff work in the Crimea, took toll in the form of thousands of deaths from exposure and disease all through the awful winter in the trenches before Sebastopol. The hospitals at Scutari and elsewhere were more dangerous to the inmates than were the trenches. The losses were appalling, and no progress was made through the winter. Assault after assault was beaten off. Napoleon, aspiring to the military fame of his uncle, was anxious to go and take command in person, and every time he made the suggestion the generals (of his own army) were panic-stricken. Matters were not going too well.

It was at this moment that Cavour stepped in— the psychological moment. Victor Emmanuel supported him, but hardly another soul did. It was the golden opportunity for the Kingdom of Sardinia to assert herself, to claim a place among the nations of Europe. She had no quarrel with Russia at all. The question of Constantinople hardly affected her; the question of the Greek church in Turkey did not affect her at all. Yet all the same she was willing to fight Russia and bolster up Turkey if that would gain her the friendship of France and England.

At the first hint of the scheme a storm of protest arose from people of all shades of political opinion in Sardinia. No one could see what profit the nation was going to obtain from the new war. If they wanted to fight anyone at all, it was Austria. There were still plenty of people who thought Sardinia could combat Austria successfully single-handed; there were plenty of others who did not think she ought to fight anyone at all. Cavour's party in Parliament lost followers from both wings, from Conservatives and Liberals. Parliamentarily speaking, he should have fallen from power and the new policy should have been discredited, but in kingdoms where the King is a man like Victor Emmanuel and the Prime Minister a man like Cavour, queer things can happen in Parliament. All possible pressure from the King was put on the deputies. Cavour spoke eloquently and managed the tactical side of the Parliamentary business with all the skill for which he was distinguished. The motion was carried, and the Kingdom of Sardinia was empowered by its deputies legally assembled to offer its help to struggling France and England.

The offer was gratefully accepted. England was experiencing some difficulty in raising men for the war—for the last time (it is to be hoped) she had been reduced to raising German mercenaries to fight her battles. The expression " ally " sounded sweeter to the ear of the English electorate than the expression " mercenary." The twenty thousand men offered by Victor Emmanuel would not, of course, be mercenaries. France was equally grateful. Although alliance with Victoria, Queen of England, was a feather in the cap of Napoleon, and showed that he really was an Emperor, he was nevertheless eager to display himself in alliance with as many other legitimate kings as possible. Besides, he had almost begun to fear that his armies might fail in their invasion of the Crimea, and that was a possibility too horrible to contemplate. Victor Emmanuel and Cavour had chosen their moment well.

Twenty thousand men was the complement decided upon. To the chief command was nominated Ferdinand, Duke of Genoa, joint hero with Victor Emmanuel of Custozza and Novara. Yet even as the appointment was made Ferdinand sickened and died.   The King was left as the last male adult representative of the House of Savoy.   Assuredly he could not go, much as he wished to.   In the end it was La Marmora, the reorganizer of the army, who was given the command of the twenty thousand men.

So they sailed to the Crimea; an Italian fleet passed the Dardanelles for the first time since the Crusades; an Italian army invaded Russian territory for the first time in history.   Not even the Romans had ever landed a military force on the Tauric Chersonese.   Victor Emmanuel waited anxiously for good news; the Opposition waited expectantly for bad.   The Royal popularity was undoubtedly passing through a period of extreme depression.

At last the good news came.   La Marmora and his men, with the French and the Turks, had won a victory.   Gortchakoff and his Russians had tried to break through to Sebastopol, and had met with a bloody reverse at the Tchernaya.   The French laughed a little up their sleeves at the Italian exultation over the victory; the English laughed much. The Tchernaya was hardly a skirmish compared with Inkermann and the Alma.   But to the Kingdom of Sardinia it was worth more even than the fall of Sebastopol.

Everyone knows Macaulay's description of the German rejoicing over Frederick the Great's victory at Rossbach.   This was a parallel case.   Never in history since the Renaissance had an Italian army won a victory over the army of another nation. Piedmontese had beaten Milanese; Venice had beaten Genoa; Italians had beaten Italians many times—too many times.   But nowhere in history could an Italian point to a pure Italian triumph. The only period before when Italians had fought united was gloomy with the names of Custozza and Novara.   The Tchernaya meant much in consequence, and Victor Emmanuel and Cavour were the men who knew best how to take advantage of it.

There were solemn Te Deums in Turin Cathedral;
there were moving speeches by Cavour in the
Chamber of Deputies. The United Italy Society
pushed the moral home dexterously through the rest of
the peninsula; Sicilians and Neapolitans, Tuscans and
Romagnols alike felt a thrill of pride at the thought
of the Tchernaya. Mazzini tried to make light of it,
as a battle won by duped Italians for a military
despot, but this action of Mazzini only further
discredited him. It was the Tchernaya which marks
the turning point in the struggle for Italian unity,
the beginning of the real ascendancy of the Kingdom
of Sardinia in Italian affairs, and the beginning
of Victor Emmanuel's popularity throughout
Italy.

In Piedmont itself the effect was immense.
Victor Emmanuel's pressure on the Lower Chamber
was forgotten; so were the severe criticisms with
which the Opposition had censured Cavour's policy.
At a bound the Royal popularity reached heights it
had never before attained. The old familiar nickname—Il Re Galantuomo[1]—which had been in
danger of being forgotten during the dark days when
he was forcing the policy upon Parliament was now
on everyone's lips.

Deft propaganda made the most of the Sardinian
successes during the rest of the war, although no
other pitched battle came to gild the laurels of the
battered battalions. La Marmora's men served
their time in the trenches; assisted a little during the
assaults; and eventually came home full of honours
—and disease. No territory had been won. Some
millions had been added to the national debt; there
were widows mourning throughout Piedmont, but
(even in the minds of many of the widows) the

[1] Probably this name was conferred upon Victor Emmanuel by
himself, as he is believed to have filled in a form for the first Sardinian
census describing his occupation as that of a " Re Galantuomo,"
but it is difficult to ascertain whether this was the first use of the
expression.

sacrifice had been worth while.   Sardinia was now a member of the concert of nations.

As such, it was represented in the conferences at Paris by Cavour, who, fortunately, had taken charge of the Ministry of Foreign Affairs when the previous holder of the office had resigned on the entry of Sardinia into the war.   Even he gained nothing substantial.   He returned to Turin, as the remnants of the Opposition bitterly pointed out, " without even a single Duchy in his pocket."   But he had managed to bring up the question of Italy for discussion by the representatives of the Powers. Those of France and England, and even of Prussia, were sympathetic and pressed for reform.   The Austrian plenipotentiary maintained a discreet silence, but this very silence displayed the impossibility of reform proceeding from Austria, and in consequence Austria was left isolated and without an ally.   What was more, channels of communication between Cavour and the Emperor of the French were now open and ready.

Meanwhile, Victor Emmanuel had not been idle. He had been active in finding further sympathy for his country, and that, too, from unexpected sources. He had succeeded in making friends with the Tsar —an amazing feat seeing that he had just made uncalled-for war upon him—partly by delicate attentions to the Dowager Empress, his mother, partly by sheer downright straightforwardness. Alexander II looked with a kindly eye on the constitutional development of Piedmont, as it made some sort of counterpoise to the power of Austria and France.

All this time Austria was in a cleft stick.   As long as liberty endured in Piedmont there would be unrest in Italy, especially in her Lombardo-Venetian kingdom.   She could not grant constitutional freedom here without granting it likewise in the rest of her dominions, and that Francis Joseph utterly refused to do. He would rather do anything else, short of losing his throne. In consequence there was continual friction between Sardinia and Austria, squabbles about extradition, about armaments, about all sorts of things, leading not infrequently to complete breaking off of diplomatic relations. And thanks to Cavour's mastery of the tactical elements of diplomatic manœuvres, Sardinia invariably appeared in the right, and Austria was repeatedly well snubbed for her pains.

Internal affairs had made considerable progress. The greatest achievement was the rendering impotent of the Jesuits, who up to quite recently had held complete control over education, and who had acted steadily as a damper upon Italian aspirations of all kinds. They had formed a rallying point for the reactionaries; now, with the new legislation, the reactionaries were practically swept away. For a brief space Cavour commanded an overwhelming Liberal majority, and he made full use of it. Free trade was the main item in his programme of financial reform, but it was not so much his free trade as the skilful energy with which he applied himself to the solution of the problems set him. He contrived to convert Napoleon III to free trade; England was going the same way. Between the three countries an intimate trade relationship sprang up, which seemed likely to swell to even greater proportions as soon as the Mont Cenis tunnel was pierced. Taxation was severe—it had to be to maintain the sort of army and navy that Victor Emmanuel wanted—but under present conditions of overflowing prosperity Piedmont was willing to be taxed, and rested supremely satisfied with her government. The improvement in the affairs of the Kingdom of Sardinia, financial, domestic, and international, compared with those prevailing in 1850, was enormous.

Just before Sardinia's entry into the Crimean

War, two deaths had relieved Victor Emmanuel of a serious clog upon his freedom of movement. Both his mother (Charles Albert's widow) and his wife were Austrian princesses, and Victor Emmanuel was notoriously susceptible to petticoat influence. In the dark days after Novara the indignant people had made much of the origin of the King's family; placards surreptitiously put up at night in Turin streets had bewailed the fact that Sardinia had an Austrian King and Queen. January and March, 1854, had witnessed the deaths of the Queen-Mother and of the Queen. In February the Duke of Genoa, Victor Emmanuel's only and much loved brother, had died. The reactionaries had almost rejoiced; they hastened to prove to the King that this series of deaths was directly due to Divine disapproval of Victor Emmanuel's attitude towards the Church. The King, sincerely religious, and harassed by father confessors and by the expostulations of Rome, was under serious strain, but in the end every one of the three deaths was advantageous to the cause of Italy. It relieved him of the need of having to justify all his actions to the women (who had repeatedly brought their influence to bear in favour of Austria), and the death of the Duke of Genoa made an end of separatist movements such as that of Sicily in 1849, when the crown had been offered to him. Victor Emmanuel was now the sole adult representative of the House of Savoy, although there was still a collateral line to which had been given the title of Savoy Carignan.

So, unhampered by financial stringency, by petticoat influence, or by skilful diplomacy on the part of Austria, Cavour began his active search for an ally who would help him make Italy. There was one close at hand, of course.

Napoleon III occupied the Imperial throne on the strength of a tradition, of several strange assumptions, and of the will of the people expressed by plebiscite. The result was that he was continually forced to show sympathy with tradition and assumptions and plebiscites.

Early in his career he had fought for Italy—his brother had died during the same campaign in which he served—the Carbonari rising of 1831 in the Papal States. He himself, some years before, had gone to some trouble to prove that his great-uncle was in favour of the doctrine of nationalities—a difficult matter to prove, seeing that Napoleon I had included Amsterdam and Rome in the same country as Paris. The theory had fitted in well with Napoleon III's statement that the Empire meant peace, which was why he had enunciated it; but since his power was based on the legend that everything Napoleon I did was right, or would have been if the rest of Europe had not interfered, it behoved Napoleon III, too, to support the doctrine of nationalities. And in Italy there was an example of a violation of this doctrine simply crying out for redress.

At the period in question Napoleon III's word was law, and his likes and dislikes were in consequence more important than any vague theory of nationalities. And here Victor Emmanuel did good work. He captivated the Emperor by his friendliness and the deference, carefully blended with independence, with which he treated him. Napoleon III had all the respect of a parvenu for blue blood and centuries of aristocratic descent. He was flattered and pleased by Victor Emmanuel's friendship.

On the other hand, Napoleon had several reasons for disliking the idea both of a united Italy and an expanded Piedmont. One of the main props of his power was the Church, and he could only be sure of the Church's support as long as he supported the Church. To the clerical mind at that period support of the Church was synonymous with support of the Temporal Power. The two ideas were then as synonymous as now they seem opposed. In a United

Italy there would be no room for the Temporal Power—both Victor Emmanuel and Pius IX made that obvious. To the aid of the Church came Eugenie, Napoleon's Empress. Eugenie had the utmost respect for Church and Pope. Sometimes she displayed it in a manner that might be misconstrued—as witness the occasion when she told Napoleon, in reply to his question as to the way to her bedroom, that " it lay through Notre Dame "— but from whatever motives, her support of the clerical party was uncompromising and determined. It was a powerful factor in the forming of Napoleon's policy.

Apart from any semi-personal considerations such as these, came the fact that in the opinion of most men a United Italy was a positive danger to France. With Italy divided, France's south-eastern frontier was unthreatened. The Pyrenees made her safe in the south, and she could devote all her attention to the Rhine—the Rhine, at which every French sovereign had cast longing eyes since the days of Philip Augustus. Consequently, the creation of trouble in Italy was a necessary factor in the French policy of pushing forward to the Rhine. A State that could mass three hundred thousand men about Chambery, within striking distance of the heart of France, would need careful watching.

In the case of war with Austria, the alliance of Piedmont could always be relied upon. The House of Savoy had no designs on Burgundy. It was purely Italian now, and only desired expansion in Italy, which meant expansion at Austria's expense. But if all Italy were brought under the rule of the House of Savoy, there was no knowing whither her ambition might lead her. She might desire additional French territory; she might—she certainly would—cast covetous eyes on the French colonies on the other side of the Mediterranean. A United Italy might be as dangerous to France as a United

Germany. Napoleon toyed with the idea—dallied with it—and then for a time discarded it.

Yet he could not put it away entirely. His conscience (and it seems quite probable that he *had* a conscience) would not leave him unreminded that on the frontier of his Empire was a divided nation. As the months and years passed after the close of the Crimean War he found that he still had to maintain an active foreign policy and keep his army—the foundation stone of the Empire—fully employed. Aggression in Belgium or Luxembourg would bring upon him the enmity of England, and friendship with the nation that had pulled his uncle from the throne was the guiding principle of his foreign policy. He could not meddle in Spain. Italy was the only possible outlet at present for his energies.

No one more keenly appreciated this fact than Victor Emmanuel, or was more aware of Napoleon's desire for military glory. He gradually grew more and more sure of success.

Suddenly terrible news came. Someone had tried to assassinate the Emperor and the Empress. The two latter, thanks to their armour-plated carriage, had escaped with scratches and bruises, but more than fifty onlookers had been killed and wounded. The would-be assassin had been taken— and he was an Italian! That, Cavour feared, would be the end of Napoleon's kindly feeling for Italy. Orsini's career was unearthed at his trial. He came from the Papal States, where he had been condemned as a conspirator. His plot had been hatched in England, but Walewski, the French Foreign Minister, insisted that he had been helped by Piedmont, clandestinely, either by the government or by private individuals. In the heat of the moment Walewski addressed a sharp note to the Sardinian government. It took all Cavour's tact to ease the situation. He disclaimed all knowledge of Orsini and his plans; he violently condemned them

in his speeches, and he rushed through the House an
Act arranging for more stringent punishment of
people who plotted against foreign potentates.
Dexterously he soothed France's injured *amour
propre*.

The effect on Napoleon was unexpected. There
was no one in the world—even including the Tsar—
whose life had been attempted more often than his.
Someone had once tried to shoot him in the Bois, and
the bullet had been stopped by the cuirass he
wore beneath his clothes.   He was surrounded by
detectives wherever he went; sentries took post on
the roofs of his palaces, and the chimneys were
guarded with wire screens, lest bombs should be
dropped down to burst on his hearth.   It was worry-
ing and annoying, and this was the last straw.
Something must be done to stop it—and there was
only one way. Italy must be pacified. He asked
Cavour secretly, " What can I do for Italy? " and
Cavour told him, speedily.

A meeting was arranged, and in dead secrecy
Napoleon came to Plombières. Cavour came too,
incognito. For two days they argued the matter in
all its aspects. Napoleon might want to pacify Italy,
but he was not averse to acquiring something for
himself in the meanwhile. He pointed out that if
Piedmont was expanded he could not afford to leave
her the passages over the Alps.   The French side
must be given to France. That meant the cession
of Savoy. Napoleon demanded Nice as well.

Now there were powerful sentimental objections
to Victor Emmanuel's cession of Savoy. It was
territory which his ancestors had ruled for over eight
hundred years; it was the territory which gave the
family its name; he himself, before his accession,
had been Duke of Savoy, and his young son Humbert
bore the same title. The sentimental objections
were far greater than would be those to the cession
of Wales by England. On the other hand, there

were not wanting hints that Savoy and Nice would prefer French rule to Italian. The population was entirely French speaking. France had always cast covetous eyes on Savoy; in 1848, when Charles Albert had invaded Lombardy, a mob of French armed civilians had occupied Chambery and proclaimed Savoy's annexation to France, although later the French government had joined with the Sardinian to force their withdrawal. Cavour was willing to yield Savoy and Nice.

Even now neither side was satisfied. Cavour had his doubts as to Napoleon III's good faith, and Napoleon III pointed out that although he was risking his dynasty and his throne by plunging into war (he had no illusions as to their ability to survive a military defeat) he personally was gaining nothing for it. He must establish himself as a member of the family of European monarchs. When, some years back, he had been looking for a wife, all the Royal families of Europe had refused alliance with him. Not merely the Kings, like Saxony and Bavaria, but even petty German States like the Mecklenburgs, had declined the honour. He had been obliged to take as his wife a private lady, one who, although in her veins (so it was said) ran the bluest blood of Spanish aristocracy, could claim no Royal descent whatever save an illegitimate one through the Duke of Berwick. It had been damaging to his prestige, there was no denying it. But he had realized that were the junior members of his house to marry Royalty, his own marriage would increase his credit. It would mean that while European Royal families were content to marry into the Bonaparte family, he himself could choose as he liked. Now he himself had a cousin Napoleon, a dissolute man of nearly forty. Victor Emmanuel had a daughter of eighteen. What could be more appropriate than a marriage between the two? Napoleon broached the subject to Cavour.

Even Cavour hesitated.   There was very little to
be said in favour of Napoleon Jerome.   He was a
man of dissolute life; he took advantage of his
Imperial relationship to pose as a democrat; his
personal courage had been impugned in the Crimean
War (where he had gained his nickname " Plon-
plon," from plomb, lead); he was erratic, untrustworthy, and uncontrollable.   Against this he could
only place his extraordinary likeness to his uncle,
Napoleon I, and his royal descent on his mother's
side from a Princess of Würtemburg.   Yet it had to
be done.   Cavour and Victor Emmanuel sacrificed
eighteen-year-old   Clothilde,   and   Cavour   and
Napoleon came to an agreement.

By the sacrifice Cavour made certain, not merely
of what gratitude Napoleon could display, but also
that Napoleon would find it harder to disavow any
participation in the secret treaty.   The marriage
would display Napoleon's intentions fully enough to
make it difficult for him to change his policy.

Napoleon had airily promised to free Italy " from
the Alps to the sea."   He bound himself to come
with his army to the aid of Piedmont in case of
attack by Austria, and in return he was promised
Savoy and Nice and the hand of Princess Clothilde
for his cousin.   The treaty was to be kept secret.

It was hardly the sort of treaty which could be
concealed, however.   Sardinia and France began
military preparations on a large scale; all over Italy
the rumour was current that great things were to
happen in the spring; the marriage of Prince
Napoleon was of course a brilliant affair; and, worst
of all, Napoleon practically made public avowal of his
intentions when, at the New Year's reception, 1859,
he told the Austrian Ambassador in the presence of
the whole diplomatic body that " he was sorry his
relations with Austria were not as good as formerly,
but it was not due to any change in his (Napoleon's)
personal feelings towards the Emperor."   That told

as plainly as any declaration of war what Napoleon intended, and it might have had serious consequences, for England was now growing restless and anxious in consequence of Napoleon's ambition, and the whole of Europe was beginning to turn a little against him. A sound diplomat at the head of Austrian affairs might have made much of this, and might have left France and Sardinia in a state of moral isolation, but there were no diplomats now in Austria. Metternich in his extreme old age had confessed as much, and had pointed out as the only diplomat in Europe the man who was planning the combination against Austria.

Austria spoilt her chances by her blundering, mad-bull diplomacy (if such a combination of noun and adjective can be tolerated). She demanded an open avowal of Sardinia's intentions. Cavour protested his innocence—the demand, of course, was not one that could expect any sort of reply. She asked the meaning of Sardinia's warlike preparations. Cavour temporized. Well-meaning Powers —England among them—stepped in and tried to preserve the peace by calling a conference. Cavour promptly agreed to the conference in principle, expressed his approval of disarmament in theory, and saw to it that mobilization quietly began. Austria was in a quandary. A conference would recommend reform in Lombardy and Venice, and she could not endure the thought of that. Worse, the conference might suggest the cession of Lombardy to Piedmont. Austria was afraid of being drawn into damaging and entangling discussions. Foiled by Cavour's diplomacy, she appealed to arms. An ultimatum to Turin demanded the demobilization and partial disbandment of the Sardinian army within three days. Sardinia of course refused, and nothing was left for Austria but to declare war. Thanks to Cavour's management, Sardinia was able to pose as the injured party, thereby making sure of the

CAMILLO DI CAVOUR

sympathy of Europe and the alliance of France, for Napoleon had declared that he could not take part in an aggressive campaign. Yet all the diplomatic success in the world would be unavailing unless supported by force of arms. The destiny of Italy once more depended on success in the field.

F

CHAPTER VI

THE NEW ENDEAVOUR

IT is necessary first to consider the field over which the campaign was to be fought. Lombardy and Venetia had now been in Austrian hands for forty-four years. Since 1848 the country had been treated like occupied enemy territory—as indeed it was. Martial law, rigorously administered, took the place of the paternal rule promised by the Austrian government during the dark days of Charles Albert's early successes. No citizen was allowed to possess arms, and martial law so construed this rule that a man was shot for being found in possession of a rusty nail. Women were flogged in the streets with Austrian officers looking on; savage punishments, torture and espionage were the order of the day. All Lombardy and Venetia were only waiting for the signal to revolt. Once indeed, Mazzini had given this prematurely. A few hundred people had risen, and a few hundred had found their way to the dungeons and the gallows.

In the Duchies—Parma, Tuscany and Modena— a similar state of affairs prevailed. In Tuscany and Parma Austrian occupation had, since 1848, taken the place of the fairly equitable rule of the earlier part of the century. And Austrian occupation invariably meant the same horrors as were prevalent in Lombardy. Modena had not enjoyed good government since the House of Hapsburg-Lorraine-Este was reinstalled in 1815; for some years since 1848 the leading man in the State was an

Englishman, Ward, who had come to Italy as His Highness's jockey and had stayed as His Highness's Minister of State.

Yet this period of horror was a blessing in disguise for Italy. Now there was no doubt in the minds of the populace as to what they would do when Austrian rule was removed. There was no thought now of erecting republics, or of organizing a constitutional government under the old rulers. The old rulers were discredited; the Republicans were discredited; there only remained the House of Savoy, which for eleven trying years had maintained constitutional government in the face of Austrian disapproval.

The Papal States were in as bad a condition as the Duchies and the Kingdom of Lombardo-Venetia. The more progressive, and (Rome excepted) the most populous part, Romagna, was in Austrian occupation. This was due to its persistent turbulence — turbulence which was continually expressing itself in demands for reform, for union with Piedmont, even (it had been this which had first begun to shake Pius IX's Liberalism) with a demand for the expulsion of the Jesuits. Expel the Jesuits from the States of the Church! A demand so preposterous must be drowned in blood. The Austrians saw that it was. So the bishops and cardinals remained in Bologna and elsewhere, backed by Austrian bayonets; in the remainder of the States of the Church the Pope's mercenary troops were able to hold down the countryside—especially as it was well known that Napoleon III would not tolerate any encroachment upon Pius's arbitrary privileges.

As soon as war began between Austria and the Kingdom of Sardinia all Italy began to make preparations for joining in. Garibaldi came to Victor Emmanuel, as he had done to his father, with offers of help. Victor Emmanuel allowed him to levy volunteers and start for the foothills of the Alps to harass the Austrian communications. Milan showed such signs of imminent revolt that the Austrian command abandoned their line through Milan and Brescia in favour of the safer but less direct one by Mantua. The Duchies showed in their attitude what would happen as soon as Austrian occupation was removed. In the Romagna the bishops informed the Austrian commander that they could not stay were the Austrian army recalled for service in Lombardy.

Yet in the midst of these troubles a great opportunity was accorded to the Austrian command. Radetsky was dead. Had he survived these few years, even to the age of ninety, or had there been anyone worthy upon whom his mantle might descend, the freedom of Italy might have been postponed indefinitely, and Napoleon III's throne might have tottered. Giulay, the Austrian commander, could have gathered his forces for one supreme effort. Evacuating Romagna and the Duchies, if need be, he could have flung himself with two hundred thousand men upon Piedmont, and Victor Emmanuel could not have opposed him with half that number. Piedmont might have been over-run even to the Alps; even Genoa might have fallen, so that French assistance would have come too late and come at a disadvantage. Austria might have held the line of the Alps indefinitely.

It was a golden opportunity, but in this campaign the hesitation and dilatoriness were, for a time at least, to be all on the Austrian side. The days passed, and the French army came streaming over the Alps or hurriedly by sea to Genoa. The Emperor came, and took over the command. He had no qualifications for the post, never having held a command in the field, and never having seen a shot fired in anger save at the Paris barricades and in the brigand warfare of 1831, but all the same he chose to take into his own hands the fates of France and Italy.

Macmahon, late commanding officer of the Foreign
Legion, the man who stormed the Malakoff and had
made the famous " *J'y suis, j'y reste* " speech on
that occasion, commanded one corps, but he was
not very much in favour because the Emperor
suspected him of Royalism. Baraguay d'Hilliers
commanded another—the man who adopted the old
Roman maxim of being sterner towards his own men
than towards the enemy. Niel and Leboeuf were
there too; and there were other names, as ominous
as that of Macmahon. Bazaine led a brigade—he
was to surrender at Metz. Bourbaki led a brigade—
he was to lead a trailing column of misery over the
Swiss frontier in the spring of 1871. But at present
no one could foresee these disasters. All was
hope and exultation, and the cheers of " *Vive
l'Empereur!* " and the brilliant uniforms—even the
Imperial Guard were there in their bearskins—might
well have led a casual observer to think that
the last Napoleon had returned to the scene of his
earliest triumphs. Yet as time went on even
the most casual observer would not have been
long deceived.

There was one ominous feature in the organization of the Imperial command. The greatest of all
the Marshals of the Second Empire was absent from
Italy. This was Pelissier, Duc de Malakoff, who
had been left behind in France. His duty was to
collect another army to make good the Rhine
frontier, in case of an unexpected attack from
Germany. Ominous it was, for it showed not only
that Napoleon was making war in Italy hampered
by having to pay attention to Germany, but it also
showed that the French military arrangements had
been inadequate and the mobilization results unsatis-
factory. Already the actual strength of the French
army was below its paper strength—Napoleon never
succeeded in bringing into Italy all the men he had
promised Victor Emmanuel.

Giulay, the Austrian commander, did worse than hesitate. He struck feebly. He pushed out a couple of reconnaissances in force—the most feeble military manœuvre possible. The officers in command, hampered and worried by their instructions not to fight a general engagement, were forced to retreat as soon as they gained contact with any force able to make a stand. At Palestro and at Montebello (where Lannes had gained his dukedom sixty years before) the Piedmontese and the French, although in vastly inferior numbers, were able to fling back the Austrian columns. The allies entered upon the serious fighting with all the prestige of two easy victories; the Austrians were depressed not only by their defeats, but by their commander's waste of opportunities.

Under Napoleon's orders the allies wheeled, basing themselves more on Turin than on Genoa. By this they gave up the advantage of making the Austrians front to a flank, and took the disadvantage upon themselves. It was a strange thing to do, yet there was a reason for it. Napoleon III had taken council with Jomini, Ney's old chief of staff, who, at the age of ninety, was resident in Paris. It was on Jomini's advice that this course was pursued; at any rate, it gave Napoleon a course of action to follow. It is doubtful whether he could devise one for himself. And so the allied armies took their weary course past Piacenza and Alessandria, across the Po, and then swung to their right to attack the Austrians beyond the Ticino. Their march was appallingly slow, for Napoleon was afraid of being surprised on the march with his columns extended. In consequence he ordered that marching should be in double columns where possible, and he insisted that the rear of every column should reach the head before a halt was made for the night. Since an army corps on the march occupies twenty miles of road, it is clearly obvious that the order bound the corps down to a kind of caterpillar mode of progression which hardly made for quick progress, and which was positively demoralizing to the supply services. An eight-mile march was a good day's work for the French army in 1859.

The country in which the allies now found themselves was flat, cut up by canals and ditches, and broken by vineyards. One great advantage Jomini's plan of campaign thus brought them : it meant that the splendid Austrian cavalry was useless. Blundering, involved infantry actions were all that were possible, and as soon as the allies began their advance they found themselves in the thick of one, around Magenta. The Austrians came groping forward; the columns met and were instantly locked in a death grapple. The battle swayed back and forth; Napoleon, in the centre of his line, knew nothing, could see nothing, could do nothing. He passed the day in feverish anxiety; his centre was repeatedly on the verge of breaking altogether. As far as he could tell, he was beaten. There seemed almost no hope of anything else. Yet success came. The struggle grew more and more tense in the centre. The French divisions, crawling slowly into action, wasted away as soon as they were thrown into the conflict. Then relief came. Far out on the left, where Macmahon had crossed the river higher up, another battle was going on, and in this Macmahon was successful. He fought his way through vineyards and across canals, until the Austrian right was gravely threatened. A Radetsky might have held on ; but Radetsky was dead. The Austrians withdrew their line a little in order to save their right, and that gave the hard-pressed French centre a breathing space. Another division came into action ; Macmahon had his men well in hand. The French flung themselves into the attack. The town of Magenta was stormed with terrible slaughter. Then, their line broken, beaten but not disordered, the

Austrian army slowly withdrew into the gathering night. Napoleon III had won his first victory.

There was no pursuit. The French army was disordered and seriously cut up. Napoleon himself was utterly exhausted with the strain and excitement of the day. Victor Emmanuel urged pursuit; Baraguay d'Hilliers, whose corps had not been in action, caught the Austrian rearguard at Melegnano and roughly handled it, but it was a despairing effort. Garibaldi led three thousand men in the north past Bergamo, raising the countryside, but he could not bring his raw levies into action against the Austrian veterans. Giulay and his men fell back unpressed to the Quadrilateral.

Napoleon was pleased with his victory, and more pleased with the way it had been won. In the excitement of the moment he had made Macmahon Marshal of France and Duke of Magenta on the field, and he saw no reason to regret this rather precipitate action. If glory and rewards would win Macmahon definitely to his side, then glory and rewards would be heaped upon him. Meanwhile, all Europe was ringing with the news of Magenta, and Napoleon pushed forward into Lombardy a recognized conqueror. Milan shrugged off the Austrian occupation with a gesture. The allied army arrived, and marched through the streets of the town, amid tossing flags and a rain of flowers, with the Milanese lining the streets and cheering wildly, drunk with their new freedom. Victor Emmanuel and the Emperor rode side by side. Perhaps the King thought of the last time he had ridden through the town, when the inhabitants were cursing his father as a traitor, when the memory of the defeat of Custozza hung heavy over the Sardinians, and he was striving in vain to collect a few men of spirit to act as rearguard to that broken army. It would be interesting to know if at that moment Victor Emmanuel thought of his dead father in his forgotten grave.

Macmahon rode in the place of honour next to Their Majesties. A little child, dazzled with excitement, came wandering out into the road among the maddened horses. Macmahon caught her up to his saddlebow for safety, and rode on with her through the rain of flowers. The little incident rang through Italy. For the moment there was in Italy no one more popular than Macmahon, unless it were his Emperor.

But despite all the cheering and rejoicing, there was still stern work ahead of the allied armies. Reinforcements from Austria came thronging down to the Quadrilateral; the Emperor himself came to take command of his white-coated battalions. Behind the fortresses of Mantua and Peschiera the Austrians rallied and reorganized, while the allies came crawling forward across the Lombard plain. They came past places famous in Napoleonic legend —Lodi and Castiglione. Then, even as they fumbled forward to the Quadrilateral, the Austrians struck. The encounter was a complete surprise to both sides. The French did not expect this offensive movement; the Austrians did not know the exact position of the French. All along the line the columns came into contact, deployed, grappled, and within an hour a long, straggling battle developed, which swayed backward and forward in front of Solferino.

Far on the left Victor Emmanuel came into contact with an Austrian corps, and was instantly locked in a struggle to the death. But the Austrian corps commander was Benedek, the best officer in the army, who seven years later was to command in chief at Sadowa. All day long this isolated struggle continued round San Martino, and it was only when evening was at hand that Victor Emmanuel was able to seize the village and force Benedek to retreat.

The decisive struggle was taking place before

Solferino. It was Napoleon III's great day. For once he had a clear idea of what he was doing, and he was able to ensure that his wishes were carried out. Quite coolly he closed the inevitable gaps which appeared in the French line during its hurried deployment. He took personal risks fearlessly. Several of his staff and of the Cent-Gardes, his personal escort, were killed in the action. Before very long Napoleon had his line well in hand and was attacking the Austrians with grim determination. The Spy of Italy, an isolated tower commanding the whole battlefield, was stormed and captured. It cost dear, though. The Austrians extricated themselves in good order; the French were shaken by their losses and badly tangled. The Austrians took up a new position round Cavriana. It appeared hardly possible for the French, exhausted by marches in the almost tropical heat, to dislodge them. The risk of attacking was enormous, and Baraguay d'Hilliers' corps, which had taken the Spy of Italy, was in no condition to renew the battle with the chances against them. It was a new invention which saved the day for the French. A year or two before Napoleon III had introduced rifled artillery into his army; it was a weapon of unknown practical possibilities, and had not had a chance to demonstrate its worth in the tangled field of Magenta. Here it was given an ideal target—massed troops on the crest of a hill, with ideal points for observation. Napoleon was an artillery man, as befitted " the nephew of his uncle," and here he had a perfect opportunity for artillery practice. The guns were ordered up. The reserve artillery and the artillery of the Guard came into action with a rush, and soon the whole Austrian line was under fire. The confusion among the Austrians was frightful; they had imagined themselves out of range, and now they had to undertake the most difficult movement of all— retirement under fire with shaken troops. It could

not be done. The retirement became a retreat.
The French pressed forward in a last effort; a
thunderstorm burst over the battlefield and added
to the confusion, and soon the whole Austrian army
was falling back. The strain of the battle had been
too great. Once on the move it was impossible to
stop them. Out on the left Victor Emmanuel sent
the Bersaglieri forward in a final effort and stormed
San Martino. Napoleon III had won his second
victory—and his last.

Once more there was no pursuit. Napoleon had
had his one day; he had risen to greatness for a
brief space, and the effort had left him neither the
will nor the strength to continue. The Austrians
had put the Mincio between them and possible
pursuit. One flank rested solidly on Mantua, the
other on Peschiera. To attack them there was to
attempt what Charles Albert had been unsuccessful
in attempting; what the great Napoleon had only
succeeded in doing with frightful exertions.

Twice had Napoleon III fought a great battle,
and each time he had only been victorious by the
narrowest of margins. Now, after the event, he was
better able to judge the result of failure. He was
convinced now that the dynasty could not possibly
stand the shock of a reverse, and he was not the man
to risk present gains for the sake of future stability.
Moreover, the strain of Solferino, and the horrible
sights and sounds of the battlefield, had altered his
outlook very considerably. As far as personal
opinion went, he would be glad to end the struggle,
and in the Empire the Emperor's personal opinion
carried as much weight as a plebiscite.

There were reasons of national policy, too.
Napoleon did not like the way matters were
developing in Italy. He had joined Lombardy to
Piedmont; but the Duchies, and Romagna as well,
were showing signs of a pressing desire to join
Piedmont as well. It would make the " Kingdom

of Northern Italy '' much too strong for his liking
if they were to do so. Yet if he were to continue
the war as Victor Emmanuel's ally, he could hardly
object to accessions of strength to that ally.   Moreover, Romagna was under Papal rule, and he would
have no hand in anything tending to a diminution
of the Papal power.

Next, it seemed as if a storm was brewing across
the Rhine. Bismarck and Von Roon had arranged
a mobilization of the Prussian army in the Rhineland. Two hundred thousand men on the French
frontier, with hardly fifty thousand between them
and Paris, were a serious consideration. He could
not find out whether the Prussian threat was a
serious one or not, but he could afford to take no
chances. The sooner he came back to Paris with
his victorious army the better.

For personal reasons, for military reasons, and
for political reasons, Napoleon was anxious to make
an end of the war. On the other side was his
promise to free Italy '' from the Alps to the sea.''
An Imperial promise was worth nothing as compared
to reasons of State. Napoleon sent a tentative
message to Francis Joseph that he might consider
an offer of peace. Francis Joseph heard, and came
anxiously to interview the arbiter of Europe, even
as his predecessor Francis I had come to interview
Napoleon I after Austerlitz. At Villafranca the two
Emperors met—Napoleon flushed with victory,
Francis Joseph borne down by strain and anxiety.
He was willing to make concessions—Hungary was
too restless for his liking. However, he was borne
up by the knowledge that Napoleon was no more
anxious for complete Italian unity than he was
himself.

The matter was settled in the course of an hour's
conversation between the two autocrats over their
coffee and cigarettes. Napoleon agreed to abandon
his ally, having won Lombardy for him. Not all

Lombardy—Mantua and Peschiera remained to Francis Joseph, so that he still held the Quadrilateral, jutting forward into the Veneto-Italian frontier, and placing Italy at a hopeless strategic disadvantage. The fragment of Lombardy in Victor Emmanuel's hands was all he was to receive; he was to restore the Duchies to their original tyrants (there was some discussion about giving Modena or Parma to Piedmont as well, but that was dropped), and in compensation the Emperors were to permit a confederation of Italy (of which Francis Joseph would be a member by right of Venetia) under the Presidency of the Pope, with a capital at Rome, a common flag, coinage and customs union. Then the Emperors made known their decisions to Victor Emmanuel.

At the news a shudder ran through Italy. The disappointment was bitter. Cavour, who had toiled and slaved for the one object of the union of Italy during ten years, broke down under it. He poured out his woes to Victor Emmanuel; he told Napoleon to his face what he thought of his shifty policy, and then flung down his portfolio and left Italy, vowing in the heat of the moment never to return. The burden of affairs fell entirely on Victor Emmanuel's shoulders, but he was equal to it. He listened to Cavour's recriminations unmoved. He already could foresee the march of events, and he knew that if only he handled the situation delicately he would be able to impose his will on the two Emperors, despite the half-million of men whom they could place in the field.

Lombardy was handed over to him. At the signature of the preliminary treaty Francis Joseph told Napoleon that he hoped it would never be his fate to have to sign away his fairest province. There was sting in the words—no Bonaparte dynasty could ever sign away a province. It would be flung from the throne as soon as there was any possibility of it.

Then the French army marched away from Italy. They went in silence—no one in Italy had a good word for the men who had only conquered one province for them. In France their reception was brilliant. All of one day they marched past the Emperor in Paris, Napoleon holding on his saddlebow the four-year-old Prince Imperial. Sedan was still ten years off.

And now began that march of events which Victor Emmanuel had foreseen, and of which he subtly took advantage. The Duchies—Parma, Modena and Tuscany—had driven out their rulers as soon as the Austrians had retired before the French. They had set up provisional governments which had promptly offered allegiance to Victor Emmanuel. He had sent representatives there to look after his interests, and, such was the nature of the temporary constitutions, these men were practically dictators responsible only to Victor Emmanuel. With dazzling promptitude plebiscites were held, and the result was almost a unanimous demand for annexation to Sardinia. Formal allegiance was offered to Victor Emmanuel, and was formally accepted. The Tuscan and Parmesan volunteers were incorporated in the Sardinian army. The whole transaction took place in a flash.

Napoleon found the ground of his objections cut from beneath his feet. He was the ardent champion of self-determination and of the theory of nationalities. His power was based on a plebiscite—the plebiscite which had followed the constitution of the Empire after the *coup d'état*. He could not send his armies to fight the man who was his recent ally; he could not object to the practice of a method he himself employed; he could not combat a theory of which he was the avowed exponent—a theory which he had laboured hard to attribute to his uncle, upon whose memory rested his power. He could do nothing except send his congratulations to Victor Emmanuel.

Nor could Francis Joseph interfere. Magenta and Solferino had weakened his armies sorely, while Sardinia was far stronger now than she had been a year ago. And he realized that France would even fight for the annexation of the Duchies to Sardinia rather than see the success bought at the price paid at Solferino nullified. Besides, England's interest in Italy was now thoroughly roused, and it was unlikely that she would tolerate armed repression of the movement—and that was the only method by which the movement could be stayed. A conference had been called at Zurich, wherein every European Power save the one most interested—Italy—was represented, for the purpose of discussing matters arising out of the peace of Villafranca. While it discussed, Victor Emmanuel acted. The Powers were confronted with a *fait accompli*, and the only means of putting back the clock was to use armed force. The only Power that wanted to fight was Austria, and Austria did not dare at present to do so.

The Romagna was the source of considerably more trouble. It had acted in a precisely similar way to the Duchies; had driven out its ruler on the withdrawal of the Austrian army of occupation; had sent troops to the aid of Victor Emmanuel; had offered him allegiance, and had received as practical dictator his representative, who in this case was Massimo d'Azeglio, Cavour's old chief, later succeeded by Farini. The plebiscite in Romagna had been as overwhelmingly in favour of annexation by Sardinia as had those in the Duchies; once again the Powers—especially France—were faced with a *fait accompli*. Napoleon was on the horns of a dilemma. He could not fight his late ally—public opinion in France would not let him—and yet he had to do something to keep the goodwill of the Pope. Napoleon was anxious to do much more to merit the

title of Eldest Son of the Church than ever its
legitimate holders, the Bourbons his predecessors,
had done. He had hoped that the honorary
Presidency of the Italian Confederation, which the
Congress of Zurich was still anxious to confer on the
Pope, would serve to placate him. But now Victor
Emmanuel, confident in the strength of his position,
would not hear of the formation of any such league,
and an Italian Confederation that did not include
the Kingdom of Italy would be but a sorry affair,
and the Presidency of it would be poor compensation
to the Pope for the loss of Romagna.

The deciding factor was the plebiscite. Napoleon
might fight the nation to which he was allied the
year before; he might quarrel with the Pope; he
might rouse all Europe in arms against him; but he
could not fight a plebiscite. With an ill grace he
submitted to the inevitable.

Victor Emmanuel had carried the matter through
by sheer audacity and accurate estimation of the
chances. He had dared much and had won much.
He had held on when even Cavour had given way.
By the force of his character he had suppressed the
last traces of the old separatist tendencies of Tuscany;
he had declined to countenance the formation of
a Central Italian State, whether a republic, or a
kingdom under the sway of a member of his family.
Thanks to his firmness and the tact of his representative, Ricasoli, who deserves to be numbered with the
great, the project had been put aside. If it had ever
been acted upon, a nearly insuperable barrier to
complete Italian unity would have been raised.

Cavour had returned to office at the beginning
of 1860, thereby admitting that Victor Emmanuel's
summing-up of the position after Solferino was more
correct than his, and his dexterous diplomacy had
done much to turn to account the vigorous energy
of the King. But he was most needed for the minor
duties of his office—the duties in which he was

most efficient. The Italian Parliament had shown
dangerous signs of disruption as soon as his dominating personality was removed; Rattazzi, his successor,
could not handle the Chamber nearly as well as he
could, and now a very ticklish matter had to be
negotiated by the Government.

Napoleon's opposition to the annexation of the
central provinces was still bitter, even if it were
concealed, and something had to be done to placate
him. At Plombières he had agreed, in consideration
for the cession of Savoy and Nice, to free Italy
"from the Alps to the sea." He had not done so.
He had given Lombardy to Piedmont, and that was
all. Yet through his actions Romagna had joined
Piedmont as well, and that meant, after all, that
Italy reached to the Adriatic as he had promised.
It was sufficient ground for him on which to base
his renewed demand for Savoy. What was more,
he had begun to ask for Savoy as a bribe for his
recognition of the annexation of the central
provinces, and he had a fair amount of right on his
side, as he was able to point out that with the
enormous increase in Victor Emmanuel's power he
must make sure that the southern frontier of France
was secure. It could never be that while Italy held
the French slopes of the Alps.

Another consideration told strongly on Cavour.
Further great events were likely to happen shortly,
and to these Napoleon must give an unqualified
approval were they to bear fruit. Mere neutrality
even would be of no avail. It must be benevolent
neutrality. Cavour wanted the whole-hearted
approval of France and of the Emperor of the
French; moreover, as he exultantly proclaimed after
the transaction was completed, it was necessary that
Napoleon III should become an accomplice in the
union of Italy. All things considered, it was for
the best that Savoy and Nice should be yielded up
to the French.

G

It was far more difficult to persuade the House of Representatives that this was so. Garibaldi was a native of Nice, and he sat in the House as deputy for his native town. And Garibaldi was already a great man, commander-in-chief of the Tuscan army, leader of an influential body of public opinion, and bitterly opposed to the cession.

A new Parliament was summoned, composed of deputies from Savoy, Nice, Piedmont, Genoa, Lombardy, Tuscany and Emilia (the new name for the united provinces of Parma, Modena and Romagna). Its first act was the approval of the annexation of the central provinces. That was easy enough—only one vote against the measure was cast in the Chamber of Deputies. Then came the tussle. Italy was flushed with success, and feeling more than a little elated and self-confident. With the memory of San Martino fresh in their minds the deputies were sure that Italy could defy France and Austria combined. That was simply absurd. French approval they must have. Once more there became observable the old familiar tactics—Cavour pleading the cause with his impassioned oratory, the King working steadily to help him behind the scenes, dexterous pressure being applied here, there, and everywhere to ensure that the Royal wishes were carried into effect. Garibaldi remained inflexible, and so did most of the other Savoyard deputies. The opposition, though numerically small, was so influential that Cavour had to yield to it to the extent of promising a plebiscite in the territories under debate. With that amendment, the measure was passed, Garibaldi and the others still voting against it.

Plebiscites are matters that can be arranged. Had a free vote been taken, it is probable that the result would have been at most a lukewarm approval of the annexation to France. As it was, Cavour's deft regulations that State officials and others who would lose by the transfer—an elastic term this—

should not vote, and the severe pressure applied from the throne, combined with the despairing indifference of the Savoyard peasantry, gained in the end a huge majority in favour of the annexation. France was placated, rendered an accomplice, and at the same time officially justified in the eyes of the world.

Officially only. France's pleasure was genuine enough. Napoleon and Eugenie made a triumphant tour through the new departments; two new jewels, representing Savoy and Nice, were added to the Imperial regalia; Napoleon's popularity reached heights that it had hardly before attained—and never was to attain again—but European disapproval of his action was widespread and profound. It showed that his motives in encouraging the Kingdom of Sardinia were not as unselfish as he would have people believe; it displayed him as a snapper-up of unconsidered trifles, and such folk are dangerous to the peace of Europe.

England, ever a little jealously afraid of France, especially when she was ruled by a man bearing the name of Napoleon, was genuinely alarmed. Napoleon's vaulting ambition was now avowed. Moreover, the English had more sympathy for Italy than for France. The annexation of Savoy and Nice, combined with the vainglorious boasting of the French army officers and the building of ironclads by the Emperor, led to a revulsion of feeling in England, previously favourable to the Empire. It expressed itself in the formation of the Volunteers, in a feverish increase in the navy, and in open denunciation in the press. Even books for children were not free of this feeling. Charles Kingsley, in "The Water Babies," gave vent to a little tirade against Napoleon III, comparing him, with a Biblical flourish, to "the man who removes his neighbour's landmark."

The affair lost Napoleon the sympathy of England; to a large degree it lost him the friendship of Italy, and it roused the suspicions of Germany. If he were so eager for little additions to his territory towards the Alps, he would not be averse to similar little additions towards the Rhine. The decline of the Second Empire dates from the annexation of Savoy and Nice.

CHAPTER VII

THE NEXT STEP

FOR ten years the Kingdom of the Two Sicilies had groaned under a despotism which was tersely described by Gladstone as " the negation of God erected into a system of Government." Ferdinand II had gained for himself the unenviable nickname of King Bomba for the ferocity of his bombardment of Messina during the rising of 1848-49. In like fashion he had dealt with all succeeding efforts, constitutional and otherwise, to obtain reform.

The government was utterly corrupt; the taxation was severe, badly distributed, and unproductive; the prisons were pesthouses crammed with political offenders. England had remonstrated gently, and had been told to mind her own business. Hints had not been wanting from France, and even from Russia, yet Ferdinand continued on his anti-national career of repression. With the moral backing of Austria and the Pope, and the assistance of an army of nearly a hundred thousand men, he was able to hold the country subservient to his will. He could not foresee the day when the power of Austria would be broken, and when his army would melt away, broken to pieces by the very forces which it was employed to combat.

Nor did he live to see it. He died in May, 1859, just after the campaign of Magenta had begun. At the beginning of the year Cavour and Victor Emmanuel had made overtures to him, offering him

101

alliance against Austria and a share of the prospective spoils. He had refused. As a matter of fact, he could do little else. Were he to declare himself on the side of Italy the spark would be set to the powder train, and the enthusiasm of the people, thoroughly roused, would wring reform from him on pain of losing his throne; and were he successful in the war there would be no Austria to help him break his promises. Sardinia and France defeated Austria unaided, while the Two Sicilies could only look on as enthusiastic neutrals. Ferdinand died as the struggle opened; he was succeeded by his son, Francis II, who proved as obdurate as his father. Perhaps the astute Bomba might have seen the trend of affairs in time to strike in and save his throne; Francis was incapable of such foresight. He remained anti-Italian, pro-Austrian, and, above all, anti-reform.

Solferino was fought and won; the Congress of Zurich began its abortive meetings; Tuscany, the Duchies, and Romagna fell to Sardinia. The Kingdom of Italy was proclaimed. Yet in Naples and Sicily there was no change. Suspects were still flung into insanitary dungeons; the import of foreign newspapers was still prohibited; the press was so censored that it might be termed non-existent; the tax-gatherers and the place-farmers still reaped their harvests.

All Italy, the Mazzinists, the party of Savoy, the plain patriots, the philanthropic party, could now turn their eyes on the Kingdom of the Two Sicilies. There were still some survivors of the days when Sicily had for nearly a year broken loose from its King, and there were still some relics of the old secret societies of that period. Crispi, who had headed the Sicilian government, and had spent ten long years in exile, was now in Italy seeking allies. In Sicily he had been able to make some slight arrangements for a rising, but a rising was hopeless unless it received help from outside.

Crispi came to Victor Emmanuel, but he was too occupied with the ticklish negotiations with France to dare to interfere in Naples. Cavour regarded him coldly, for he was of the party of Mazzini, an old Republican, and probably still tainted with separatist tendencies. Yet Crispi, nowise daunted, still sought for help, and he went to the man who could most easily give it.

Farini was the dictator of Emilia—Victor Emmanuel's man, yet ostensibly still independent of him while the fate of Emilia hung in the balance. He was willing to help Crispi, and he gave the kind of help which was of most use. He pledged the government of Emilia to a subsidy of two million francs, and he enlisted the help of Garibaldi. Cairoli, Bixio, and the others—Carbonari, revolutionaries, exiles, but hard fighters and desperate plotters all of them—came to Modena and took part in the conferences. Garibaldi wavered. There had been too many unsuccessful revolts in the Two Sicilies for any man to enter into the attempt with a light heart —failure meant further slaughter and torture and pillage in the unhappy province. Farini was willing to take the risk. If he were unsuccessful, Victor Emmanuel could disavow him, and he would be discredited in the eyes of all Italy. If he were successful, Victor Emmanuel and Garibaldi would take all the credit. His evident disinterestedness, Crispi's urgings, and some secret messages of approval from Turin eventually decided Garibaldi to make the attempt.

Garibaldi was the ideal leader of men. His defence of Rome, his marvellous retreat across Italy, and his achievements at the head of his volunteers in the late war had given him a prestige that no other popular leader could match. At a whispered word from him a thousand of his old " redshirts," his volunteers, began to assemble in Genoa. They knew that they were destined for a desperate

enterprise; it was almost universally known that that
enterprise was to be aimed against the relentless
Neapolitan Bourbons; but they were willing to follow
Garibaldi wherever he might choose to lead them.
Farini's two million francs secured for them two old
steamers lying in Genoa harbour, the *Piemonte*
and the *Lombardo*.   Rattazzi, Victor Emmanuel's
Minister of the Interior, promised arms, and then
found himself unable to provide them.   It was a
serious check, but Garibaldi, now that his heart was
in the movement, was not to be turned back.   There
were some mysterious negotiations with Ricasoli,
the Commissioner for Tuscany, and then the two
steamers set sail.

They turned unexpectedly into Orbetello, where,
by a strange coincidence, Ricasoli had left an
unguarded store of arms.   The store was raided, and
all the weapons confiscated by Garibaldi; curiously,
the Tuscans offered no objections.   Then they
continued on their course for Sicily.   Francis of
Naples knew by now whither they were bound, and
the Sicilian navy was charged to sink the steamers on
sight, but they did not catch sight of them until too
late.   The course was well chosen; a great part of
the navy was not too enthusiastic, and the *Lombardo*
and the *Piemonte* were close inshore near Marsala
and the thousand were nearly all landed before two
Sicilian frigates hove in sight.   Close at hand were
two British ships of war.   England was at peace with
Naples; her ships might almost have acted legally in
firing into Garibaldi's steamers as common filibusters,
but England was far too sympathetic towards the
popular cause for anything like that to happen.
Instead, the British ships came up near the rebels,
and the Sicilian commander, daunted by the thought
that perhaps England was in league with Garibaldi,
and that any hasty action on his part might lead to
open war between the two countries, held back until
the landing was completed.

Garibaldi marched his thousand into the interior, and promptly proclaimed a provisional government, with himself as Dictator and Crispi Minister of State. In addition, he boldly announced that his intention was to conquer Sicily for Victor Emmanuel. It was not an easy statement to make. Garibaldi was at heart a Republican, as befitted the defender of Mazzini's triumvirate, but he knew that the Powers of Europe still looked askance at Republican movements, and he knew, too, that he could only hope at best for tolerance from Victor Emmanuel were he not to act on his behalf. Moreover, the union of Italy was as dear to Garibaldi as were any theoretical principles of government, and he could see now that were not Italy united under Victor Emmanuel she would never be united at all.

So Victor Emmanuel was proclaimed, and the Sicilians came flocking in to join Garibaldi. If they did not want to fight for Victor Emmanuel—and most of them did—they still wanted to fight against the Bourbons, and here was the chance of a lifetime. The Royalist army moved out against them, hesitated, though nearly twice as strong numerically, fell back, and then entrenched themselves at Calatafimi. Garibaldi marched to attack them. He attacked three times, and was successful at the last attempt, although the losses he suffered were appalling. The Neapolitans fell back, were heavily reinforced, and again entrenched outside Palermo. Garibaldi gathered together all his strength, attacked and was beaten back. The insurgents poured out their blood like water, but to no purpose. Then Crispi came to the rescue. Thanks to his experience as a hunted rebel he knew of by-paths which turned the Royalist position. Garibaldi acted on the knowledge like lightning, slipped away from the Neapolitan front, and, while the Royalists searched for him in fumbling fashion in the hills he suddenly appeared in their rear, assaulted Palermo, and had the city in his power before his late opponents could return. The city rose for him, but he still had to fight the garrison of the citadel and the returning Neapolitan army. The citizens were of little use in the fighting; the Neapolitan fleet and the citadel combined in bombarding the place (the tradition of Ferdinand II still bore fruit), but Garibaldi by sheer force of personality was able to beat back the Royalists and hold on to the town. Just when his ammunition was exhausted the nerve of the Neapolitan commander failed him, and an armistice was proposed. Garibaldi reached the summit of his audacity. He demanded immediate evacuation of town and citadel on pain of the instant slaughter of the garrison. He would give no quarter, he declared —every man in the place who held for King Francis would be put to the sword. It was a bold declaration to make, seeing that he was outnumbered, his men were worn out, and his ammunition was completely exhausted. Yet it saved the cause of Sicily. The Neapolitan commander was completely cowed. He surrendered the place, transferred his men to the fleet, and sailed away to the mainland.

As soon as this conspicuous success had been achieved, the Neapolitan occupation of Sicily fell to pieces. Garrisons were hastily withdrawn; a despairing plan of campaign was drawn up but was not adhered to—for Garibaldi was not the man to give his enemy time to rally. He dashed upon Milazzo, fought a furious battle, and captured the place. Messina fell into his hands without resistance—a convention neutralizing the garrison of the citadel. All Sicily fell promptly into his hands.

Francis II was seriously alarmed. He wrote indignantly to his fellow monarchs demanding that this assault upon legitimacy should be beaten down. Nobody listened to him. The British Minister for Foreign Affairs circularized his ambassadors frankly approving of all that was going on; Austria was

GUISEPPE GARIBALDI
MONUMENT AT ROME

too weak to help; Napoleon III hesitated. Francis
even asked for help from Victor Emmanuel—to be
reminded that he had refused help a year before. He
tried to consolidate his waning power in Naples.
He promised a constitution, but his father before
him had promised constitutions, and obliterated them
later in blood. All Europe, as a matter of fact, was
amused that retribution was at last descending upon
the Neapolitan Bourbons.

To Garibaldi in Sicily help came from all Italy.
Volunteers flocked to him; money poured in in
streams. Victor Emmanuel gave countenance now
to the attempt, and Garibaldi was able to gather a
considerable force, nearly twenty thousand men,
about Messina. With this army he crossed the
straits and landed in Calabria. Francis could oppose
him with eighty thousand, and his best course, had
it been possible, would undoubtedly have been to
march at once upon Garibaldi. But the Neapolitan
army, rotten with treason, and now displaying all the
results of ten years' peculation and bad treatment, was
in no condition for offensive movements. It might
fight, but it could not march. Certainly it would
not fight with the largest city of Italy smouldering
with rebellion in its rear. Francis abandoned Naples
to Garibaldi and fell back upon the Volturno, a
strong position backed by the almost impregnable
fortress of Gaeta. Garibaldi marched into Naples,
in the midst of scenes of tremendous enthusiasm.
The people filled the streets cheering madly, and yet
as soon as the news spread that the conqueror was
lying down, worn out, and trying to snatch an hour's
sleep, they quietened instantly, standing silent in the
square all through the afternoon.

From Naples Garibaldi issued proclamations,
naming himself Dictator, giving the command of the
Neapolitan fleet (which had come over to him) to
Persano, the Piedmontese admiral, and declaring
that he would make no compromise with the

Bourbons. For Francis had made him offers. He had suggested that Garibaldi should receive two million sterling to leave him alone, and the help of the Neapolitan army so that he could go and worry someone else—Austria, whose retention of Venetia was known to be exasperating to him. Yet two million sterling—the most princely bribe ever offered to a private individual—had no attraction for Garibaldi; as for the Venetian scheme, Garibaldi had other plans. All he wanted at the moment was to get rid of the Bourbons. He declined the offers, and led his men to the Volturno. Here he was for the time doomed to failure. The Neapolitans fought with determination in their entrenched position, and Garibaldi was beaten back, despite all his determined efforts. The freedom of Naples was being dearly bought. Garibaldi was at the end of his tether apparently; he could not drive Francis from the Volturno, and yet failure was dangerous. Rebellious movements can only thrive on success. However, help was now close at hand, but before the description of the conquest of Naples can be continued it is first necessary to examine the relations existing between Victor Emmanuel and the Papacy.

CHAPTER VIII

THE CHURCH AND THE NATION

PIUS IX had set his face, ever since the events of 1849, against any movement towards reform or union. He became more repressive than Austrian or Bourbon. On his return from Gaeta, reinstated by the French and Austrian armies, he had abolished the reforms granted in the early Liberal years of his tenure of office, and had re-established priestly rule throughout his dominions. The taxes were, as always, unbearably severe, unequitably levied, and badly collected. It is impossible to speak of the administration of justice —justice was never administered. Injustice was meted out under archaic legal forms; the evidence of police was always accepted against that of private people; confessions to accusations were wrung from suspects by torture. It was as treasonable to discuss the possible union of Italy as it was to suggest reform. Pius had absolutely refused to help Sardinia against Austria in 1859; had he dared, he would have sent his army against Victor Emmanuel. As it was, he was helpless. He knew, once Austria was defeated, that his sole means of retaining his temporal power was by the assistance of France. His armies could not oppose for a moment the armies of Victor Emmanuel. When the Romagna revolted he was unable to raise the military force necessary to subdue the country—he could not use French troops, seeing that the Romagna had declared itself in alliance with

France. It has already been related how in the
end Romagna and the Duchies were annexed to
Piedmont. Against such a settlement Pius naturally
declared himself uncompromisingly. In the official
journals of Rome he denounced Victor Emmanuel's
actions; he raged against him; he launched a bull of
excommunication against him.

Victor Emmanuel tried by soft answers to turn
away his wrath; the Christian nature of his replies,
however, failed in their effect upon the Head of the
Church. The King humbly pointed out that matters
were beyond his control, that it would be as much
as his throne was worth to try to restore Romagna,
and he hinted, deferentially, that if the Pope were
to set about bringing order into his dominions he
would find that revolts were not so frequent. The
Pope paid no heed. Instead, he saw to it that
further revolts would not find him unprepared. He
began to collect an army. Napoleon III highly
applauded the project; he would be glad to see a
power arise in Italy to counterbalance Victor
Emmanuel's growing strength. For commander-in-
chief Pius selected Larmoricière, the best of the
French officers who had left their country at the
time of the *coup d'état*. Fervent Catholics all over
Europe were called upon to enlist in the Papal army
and aid in the repression of Liberalism. A thousand
or two came. Napoleon did his best to help. Any
of his men who wished to join the Pope was at once
given long leave; pressure was applied to compel
officers to avail themselves of the opportunity. In
a short time Larmoricière was at the head of a
large but motley army—of Frenchmen, Belgians,
Bavarians, Italians, Austrians, badly equipped (the
Cardinal in office showed no aptitude for the business
of Minister of War), and, despite Larmoricière's
heroic efforts to make the most of the time allowed
him, badly trained.

Army or no army, Pope or no Pope, the Papal

States were in a condition of profound agitation. Misgovernment, the formation of the Kingdom of Italy, and the successful revolt of the Romagna, all combined to raise the excitement to fever heat. Umbria and the Marches were in a ferment. There were one or two demonstrations and attempts at revolt. Larmoricière put them down.

Victor Emmanuel, with his army massed on the Papal frontier, was watching developments keenly yet anxiously. He was too sincere a Catholic to treat his quarrel with the Pope lightly. Yet he saw no way of reconciling his duty to the Church with his duty to Italy. Perhaps he was convinced that he imperilled his soul by freeing Italy contrary to the will of the Pope. Such a consideration would have weighed with his father; with Victor Emmanuel the case was different. If the unification of Italy could be bought at the price of his damnation, that price he would be willing to pay.

Affairs were very tangled. Cavour could never forget that Garibaldi was one of Mazzini's disciples. Despite the proclamation of Victor Emmanuel by Garibaldi in Sicily and Naples, he was still darkly suspicious that the proclamation was only issued to allay European distrust while Garibaldi strengthened his hold on the Two Sicilies, until he would be able to proclaim himself Consul, or Triumvir, or give himself some other highflown title, and set up in the south a republic which, by its very nature, would be compelled to act in continual antagonism to the Kingdom of Italy in the north. Cavour vented his suspicions to Victor Emmanuel with such point and frequency that the latter, against his will, came to some extent to share them. Moreover, Garibaldi was openly proclaiming that Naples and Sicily would not content him. Rome must come next, and after that Venice. Such headstrong recklessness would plunge the infant kingdom into simultaneous war against both France and Austria. Victor Emmanuel could not stand by and allow such a thing to happen.

In addition to these considerations was the knowledge that Garibaldi was expending his strength without result against the Neapolitan positions at Capua and on the Volturno, while Larmoricière's Papal army was increasing every day in numbers and efficiency. If the Papal army were sent against Garibaldi—as well it might be—there was no foreseeing the result. Garibaldi might easily be beaten, and the Bourbons would come into their own again. Victor Emmanuel could only choose between fighting the Pope or leaving affairs entirely in Garibaldi's hands. In Sicily Garibaldi's conduct was, from a casual inspection, at least equivocal. Victor Emmanuel had been proclaimed, and a royal commissioner sent to the island, but Crispi, Garibaldi's Minister of State, clung to the reins of power. Both he and Garibaldi wished to hand the island over to the House of Savoy only by slow steps. They wanted a large degree of autonomy for Sicily; and to a certain extent they were right, for Sicily was quite a different country from the rest of Italy, with different traditions, with a continual desire for autonomy, and with the thought of Bentinck's administration of 1812 and of the year of freedom of 1848 still green in the memory of the people. Crispi wanted to educate the people to constitutional government, and then to induce them to enter voluntarily into constitutional union with Italy; but nothing short of annexation would satisfy Victor Emmanuel. Any voluntary engagement would necessarily imply the reservation that Sicily could at will rescind her allegiance. With the Duchies and Lombardy Victor Emmanuel could be sure that such a thing could never happen. With Sicily he could not be sure, especially as the conflict of wills between his commissioner and Crispi was leading already to a dangerous state of tension. So, of the two courses

open to him—of war with the Pope or leaving
Garibaldi a free hand—Victor Emmanuel inclined
towards war with the Pope.

Yet such a war was not at all to his taste.
Rather than have to enter upon it, he was prepared
to make considerable sacrifices. He would be
content with the cession to himself of Sicily by
Ferdinand, leaving the mainland to the Bourbons,
and without interfering further with the Papal States.
Garibaldi would not hear of it. Nothing less than
Naples and Sicily would satisfy him. He even went
so far as to demand the dismissal of Cavour, who
had suggested the compromise. It was clear now
which was the lesser of the two evils. As the Papal
attitude became more and more menacing, Victor
Emmanuel boldly dared the wrath of France and
Austria and demanded the disbandment of the Papal
army, which was tersely described in his proclamation as " suffocating every expression of national
sentiment." Pius refused; he put his trust in
Larmoricière's army and in the support of
Napoleon III. It would be hard to say which was
the more untrustworthy ally.

There was nothing left now save to declare war.
Victor Emmanuel gave the word, and his two
armies, which had been straining at the leash on the
Papal frontier, plunged headlong into Umbria.
Larmoricière moved his motley mass of crusaders to
meet them, but it was dashed utterly to pieces at
Castelfidardo. Larmoricière, riding headlong from
the field, brought the news of his own defeat to
Ancona, as Sir John Cope did to Dunbar. He tried
to gather the wreck of his forces together there for
one last effort, but Cialdini, following up with the
utmost determination, hemmed him in, and forced
him to surrender on pain of assault and sack.
Larmoricière, a good soldier in a bad cause, badly
supported, came back to Rome, resigned his commission into the hands of the Pope, and withdrew.

H

Pius bore him no malice for his failure, and offered him considerable rewards. He refused them, and retired into private life to nurse the bitterness of defeat.

Meanwhile, Cialdini overran Umbria and the Marches, and, pressing forward by forced marches, reached Neapolitan territory. Victor Emmanuel followed after at a more dignified pace. The breach between himself and the Pope now gaped more widely than ever—it was a breach which now could never be healed. Pius was furious at the loss of two-thirds of his dominions. He was in a frenzy of anxiety in case the King should carry his disrespect for the Head of the Church so far as to attack Rome itself. In all his official utterances he denounced Victor Emmanuel's actions and intentions. He cut him off from the Church. Had he had his way, the Italians would have risen in rebellion against him. Fortunately, he was so utterly discredited politically that Italians paid no heed to his political pronouncements. They still revered him as the Vicar of Christ, but they had only contempt for him as a temporal ruler or as a politician. They contrived somehow to reconcile their duty to their King with their duty to the Church—or if they could not, then they held to their duty to the King. Victor Emmanuel was in no danger from Pius' political machinations.

Napoleon III, however, was witnessing these new developments with consternation. At Villafranca he had said with a sneer, " Let us now see what the Italians can do for themselves "—alluding to Charles Albert's historic " *Italia farà da se*." Now he was indeed seeing what the Italians could do. They had turned the Bourbons out of Sicily, had conquered nearly all Naples, had beaten the army which he had had considerable share in raising for the Pope, and had conquered Umbria and the Marches, all within the space of a few months. If he still wanted a divided Italy he must act at once with all his strength, and that was exactly what he could not do.

Brute force alone would reconquer the Two Sicilies for Francis, and Umbria for Pius. In the former case, it was manifestly absurd for a Bonaparte to fight to regain a throne for a Bourbon—it would be a bad example for the people who had displaced a Bourbon in his favour in 1848. Besides, French public opinion was entirely on the side of Garibaldi. His success with the thousand was strongly reminiscent of Napoleon's conquest of France before the Hundred Days, while the abominations of the Bourbon rule were known to all the world. Moreover, England was unequivocatingly on the side of freedom. Napoleon's entry into the affair on the other side would lose him what little goodwill he still retained on the other side of the Channel. It might conceivably even lead to war. And war with England was more than Napoleon could face—to say nothing of the fact that at the first hint of it for such a purpose he would probably lose his throne. So he could only do his best in an underhand fashion, and underhand methods were ineffective against downright activity like Garibaldi's and Victor Emmanuel's. He could advise Francis; he could send his fleet with sealed orders to cruise on the Neapolitan coast; he could bluster and threaten, but he could do nothing effective.

In the case of Pius, his position was a little stronger. France might conceivably fight for the Pope, and England had not so much objection to Papal rule in Rome as to Bourbon rule in Naples. Thanks to the French garrison in Rome, there were no demonstrations against Pius in the Patrimony of St. Peter—the little area of Rome and its environs. So Napoleon could not be confronted with a *fait accompli* here as he had been elsewhere. To turn the Pope out of Rome, or to hold a plebiscite in Rome, would involve, as a necessary preliminary, fighting with the French garrison—and once there was fighting, and the French national honour was touched, Napoleon would be able to lead the French people into a war to the knife with Italy. The general opinion was that, were this to happen, he would win; Magenta and Solferino had raised his army to a pitch of enthusiasm and efficiency which, although decline was soon inevitable, made him a dangerous opponent. Victor Emmanuel could do whatever he liked as long as he only offended Napoleon. He dared do nothing to offend France.

As a matter of fact, it is difficult to see what the King could have done other than what he did do. All Italy was watching Garibaldi, and when he was beaten back at the Volturno all Italy demanded that Victor Emmanuel should go to his aid. The fact that he could only do so by marching across Papal territory and fighting the Papal army only made Italy the more desirous that he should. Victor Emmanuel might have resisted this popular demand, as he had resisted others, but it might well have cost him either his throne or the Kingdom of the Two Sicilies. The tremendous rapidity with which the Italian affair developed forced his hand. He himself would rather that events had moved more slowly and with greater difficulty—it would have been for the eventual good of the country had they done so—but as it was he was compelled to act at once.

With Umbria and the Marches in his power, and his armies thrusting forward into Neapolitan territory, he asked Parliament whether it approved of the annexation of these two provinces and of the whole Kingdom of the Two Sicilies. The reply was overwhelmingly in the affirmative, and, backed by this mandate, Victor Emmanuel entered Naples to hunt down the lion whose skin had thus been disposed of beforehand. It was a matter of some difficulty. At his approach, with the powerful Italian army at his back, Francis abandoned his position on the Volturno, which he had held against all Garibaldi's assaults. Capua was taken, and Francis took refuge in his last fortress, Gaeta. Here he was closely besieged, but the operations of the besiegers were hampered by the ambiguous attitude of Napoleon III, who withdrew his minister from Turin and sent his fleet to lie in Gaeta harbour. The King gave orders that the siege was to be pressed as closely as possible under the circumstances, without damaging French ships, and then turned to consolidate his new kingdom.

He made a triumphant entry into Naples with Garibaldi at his side. A plebiscite taken in the dual kingdom gave an overwhelming majority in favour of annexation to Italy, and arrangements were immediately pushed forward for the election of deputies from the new provinces to the Parliament of United Italy. It was here that party politics began their dislocating influence in Southern Italy.

The relations between Cavour on the one side and Garibaldi and Crispi on the other were badly strained. Cavour could never get over his prejudice against the other two as Mazzini's men; Garibaldi could never forgive Cavour for his cession of Savoy and Piedmont. Both Garibaldi and Crispi were convinced, in their heart of hearts, that the Republican form of government was the best in theory, and Cavour knew that they were. He could not make sufficient allowance for the fact that at the same time they realized that in Italy submission to Victor Emmanuel was the best course in practice. Moreover, Crispi's high-handed methods in Sicily (he even at one period put the Royal Commissioner under arrest) roused Cavour's suspicions. Garibaldi had demanded Cavour's dismissal at the time of the compromise proposals to Francis II. Cavour was jealous of Crispi's evident talents and political genius, as well as of his personal popularity. Garibaldi thought Cavour timid because he picked

his steps carefully, avoiding as far as possible any
offence to France or Austria; he himself would have
marched on Rome and Venice without a thought.

Victor Emmanuel's arrival at Naples did a little
towards easing the situation. He took over
Garibaldi's dictatorial powers, thus relieving him
from two temptations which must have pressed him
sorely. One was to retain his personal power over
Naples; the other was to march on Rome. But his
good sense and inherent loyalty won the day. He
handed over to the King and went into retirement.
He refused all titles, honours and rewards, as he had
refused Francis II's two millions, but it is to be
suspected that his annoyance with Cavour had something to do with this. However, it was as well that
he did so. Garibaldi as Duke of Messina or Prince
of Caprera would no longer have been Garibaldi.
He was removed from Cavour's path; the President
of the Council was now free to come to grips with
Crispi.

Cavour had the King's influence (probably
exerted without Victor Emmanuel's knowledge) to
help him. In the new elections that influence was
exerted to the full. All things were possible in the
election; Cavour saw to it that everything that
happened was in his own favour, as far as the
control lay in his power. His influence was such that
he actually contrived to arrange for Crispi's defeat at
the polls at Palermo—the town which idolized
Crispi. However, Cavour's power was not universal.
Even in enlightened Italy, with its brand new
parliamentary apparatus, there were such things as
pocket boroughs. As member for one such, Crispi
entered the new Italian Parliament, vowed to eternal
enmity against Cavour.

The siege of Gaeta dragged on. The last
remnants of the Bourbon army fought valiantly, and
while the sea remained open it seemed impossible
that anything effective could be done. Victor

Emmanuel did not want to assault—baptism in Italian blood would be a bad start for the infant kingdom. However, Napoleon's " faultering boldness " gave way in the end, and he took away his fleet. The harbour was promptly blockaded by the Italians, and the fall of Gaeta became inevitable. Francis II saved Victor Emmanuel the trouble of having to dispose of a prisoner of royal pretensions. His sister was Maria Christina, Queen of Spain, and she sent a naval escort for him. Guarded by a Spanish frigate, he went by sea to Rome. Victor Emmanuel was glad to see the back of him, and Gaeta promptly surrendered. All Italy was now in the hands of Victor Emmanuel, save for Venetia and Rome. The exceptions were important—the question of Rome, especially, seemed likely to split the newly-erected edifice to the foundations. Nevertheless, there was now a Kingdom of Italy, and a constitutional kingdom at that. The achievement was one to be proud of.

CHAPTER IX

THE MEN RESPONSIBLE

THE names of four men are indissolubly connected with the history of the union of Italy. They are Victor Emmanuel, Garibaldi, Mazzini and Cavour. Up to the present the narrative of events has proceeded so tumultuously and breathlessly that there has been no opportunity of discussing the comparative claims of these four to the glory of the final achievement, but now, with Italy nearly united, and with the principal actors already beginning to vanish from the stage, the question may in part be answered.

Mazzini was the eldest of the four, and he was the one who was earliest involved in efforts against the Italian despots. In fact, it was the despots he disliked—not disunion. In the beginning he had been a Carbonaro, and although in the decline of that society he renounced his membership, a Carbonaro he remained to the end of his life. Freedom to him was impossible under a constitution which recognized kingship. He conspired against Austria, against the Pope, against Charles Albert in his early repressive period. Exiled from Italy as a matter of course, he maintained a steady flow of propaganda into the country. In the business of propaganda he was supreme; there was no one to compare with him in ability to rouse enthusiasm. Where he was deficient was in the ability to direct that enthusiasm. He was the worst plotter in

MAZZINI

history.   Possibly his plots were deliberately laid so
that they might fail; he thought, rightly, that the
more blood that was spilt the higher the feeling that
would rise.   But it was a wasteful and extravagant
plan of campaign, if indeed it were his plan.

He was never able to realize that the key to the
Italian difficulty lay in Sardinia; blinded by his
hatred of monarchy he was prepared to bring upon
his head and upon the heads of his followers the
displeasure of Cavour and Victor Emmanuel.   He
scorned the help of fifty thousand Sardinian soldiers,
and instead he only gained the help of a few hundred
Italian peasants.   Garibaldi, it is true, conquered a
kingdom with the aid of a thousand soldiers, but he
would never have succeeded without the assistance of
Victor Emmanuel.

Mazzini's political foresight was as deficient as
his ability to plot.   The rise of Victor Emmanuel
surprised him as much as it annoyed him.   He
looked to see the Italy of the future a republic,
freed by her own exertions from Austria and France.
It was these chimerical ideas—they certainly were
chimerical, for never in the last century was there
the least chance of an enduring republic in Italy—
which led him to the formation of the Roman
Republic, which encouraged him to veto Garibaldi's
bold plan of marching on Naples at the approach
of the French troops in 1849, and which led him to
organize the revolt, criminal in its lack of preparation, at Milan in 1853.   An examination of the
details of this last conspiracy displays Mazzini's shortcomings as a plotter.   He was sure of the help of
about two hundred men; the Austrian garrison was
nearly twenty thousand.   Yet he hoped that the
population would rise, that they would forget the
awful lesson of 1849, and that, having driven out
the Austrians, they would act as a rallying point
for revolutionaries throughout Europe—including
Sardinia, so that Poland and Prussia would owe

their freedom to the example of a single town in Italy.   The proclamations he had printed in readiness for the rising tell of this at great length.

Mazzini planned the rising with that elaboration of detail which displays the unskilful plotter.   There were eighteen men stationed at the main guard of the citadel; eighteen rebels were told off to assassinate them exactly at five o'clock in the afternoon. Radetsky and his brother generals, who were to dine together at the Palace, under military guard, were to be murdered by a hundred others.   A few more were to rouse the people in the streets to murder the Austrian officers and men likely to be walking there. Pickaxes and crowbars were to be at hand for the erection of barricades.   Klapka, one of Kossuth's generals, was to try to seduce the Hungarian regiments of the garrison.   The whole elaborate scheme was to come into action at a prearranged signal.   The signal was given; Mazzini was waiting anxiously on the Swiss frontier for news; the rebellion fizzled out like a damp squib.   No one could reasonably have expected the populace, drastically disarmed by Radetsky, and with the memory of 1849 still fresh in mind, to have risen in such a desperate effort.   Some two hundred conspirators appeared; they captured a couple of guns and made some slight resistance, but the whole affair was over in an hour. Ten Austrians were killed and wounded; some twenty rebels were captured and executed and nearly a hundred were flung into prison, to remain there until 1859.   The Hungarian regiments, whose presence six years later might have been invaluable, were sent back to Austria.   More harm was done than good.

And yet, despite these shortcomings, Italy owes much to Mazzini. It was his society of Young Italy which first made a definite effort to express Italian aspirations.   It was Young Italy which kept the embers glowing through the dark days of Charles

Albert's reactionary measures. The Roman episode, although it was only an episode, was nevertheless one which would make any Italian heart swell with pride. Mazzini gave Garibaldi his first opportunity to distinguish himself in Italy—Charles Albert had the chance before him and had declined it. Mazzini was not deterred from any project by his respect for King or Pope or Emperor—rather the reverse. It is doubtful if Italy could have thrown off her submission to the Pope so readily if it had not been for Mazzini. To his writings is largely due English sympathy with Italy, and English sympathy was a powerful factor in the unification.

Mazzini's very mistakes were helpful. If he had not insisted on a republican constitution for the Central States, it is quite possible that they might have coalesced into a stable constitutional monarchy, and the union of Italy would then have been postponed indefinitely. If he had not pressed so frantically for Utopian reforms, Italy might not have come to realize the practical blessings of Victor Emmanuel's government. If he had not declared himself at enmity to Victor Emmanuel, there would have been no reaction after 1849 in favour of Savoy. Mazzini was an indispensable adjunct to the movement. He was the voice to which Europe outside Italy listened; he was the irrepressible spirit which was undaunted by any reverse. He supplied the extra energy to convert unrest into rebellion.

The second of the four, Garibaldi, was the sledge-hammer which did the welding together of Italy. Generally he was guided by others; and generally when he was not his blows fell at the wrong time or place. He was indispensable, too. He brought into Mazzini's counsels a steadying balance of practical military experience, and when he decided that a scheme was practicable he spared neither himself nor his men to bring it to fruition. Untiring, with a vast personality, full of resource and of the very

highest courage, he was the ideal leader of partisan
and guerrilla warfare.   No one but he, not Napoleon
himself, could have freed Sicily from the Bourbons
as he did.   There is hardly a feat of arms in history
worthy to rank with the brilliant flank movement and
long weary march with beaten men from Monreale
to Messina.   It was the one possible way to convert
defeat into victory.   Garibaldi thought of it.   It was
terribly difficult.   Garibaldi overrode the difficulties.
It called for high courage and the ability to
stimulate the failing spirits of the men.   Garibaldi
had the courage and the ability.   His reputation,
based on the tales his men told of his feats in South
America, and on the more substantial foundation of
the memory of his retreat from Rome, in the wild
march when he outwitted a kingdom and an empire,
was worth more to Italy than twenty thousand men.
To Crispi in the Sicilian expedition he owed much;
it was Crispi who prepared the ground for him, and
who made all the arrangements in the island itself.
Crispi drafted proclamations and constitutions.   It
was even Crispi who at the crucial moment found the
way past the Neapolitan flank at Monreale.   But it
was Garibaldi who carried it through.   One of
the handsomest men in Europe, with his golden
beard flying and his eyes blazing, he led wherever
there was danger, and wherever he led his men
followed.

His loyalty was of as much value as his vigour and
his skill.   He must have been sorely tempted when
he found a kingdom in his sole power.   Such was his
prestige that he might have ruled the Two Sicilies
himself, independent of Victor Emmanuel, but he
knew that any such attempt would damage the cause
of Italy irreparably, and it was of Italy that he
thought.   It would be ignoble to speculate as to how
much he dallied with the temptation—Crispi's advice
must have worked powerfully on him, and he must
have been disappointed when he found Cavour

determined on setting aside their cherished scheme of educating the Sicilians and Neapolitans by slow degrees to a sufficient political intelligence to justify their inclusion in the Italian electorate.

With the guidance of someone of acute political insight, Garibaldi was an immense power. It was when he had to act on his own initiative that his sledgehammer blows were misdirected. After 1860, he was of less use to Italy. He could not appreciate Victor Emmanuel's difficulties at all. He was willing to sacrifice himself, to be made the scapegoat if need be; he could not see that it was highly undesirable that there should ever be need of a scapegoat. Exasperated in the end so that his good sense deserted him, he tried to force Victor Emmanuel's hand—to find that Victor Emmanuel was more skilful at that process than he was.

But he gave Italy an example, an ideal, and a history. By the strength of his arm he cut Gordian knots indissoluble even to Victor Emmanuel. He established a tradition of disinterested patriotism which later Italian politicians would have done well to observe. He secured for Italy independence without compromise—more than any of the other makers of Italy hoped for, at that time at least. Because of Garibaldi the expression " constructive warfare " is no longer a contradiction in terms.

Cavour was the statesman, as opposed to the plotter and the soldier. He owed duty to the Kingdom of Sardinia as well as to Italy in general to a greater degree than even Garibaldi thought necessary; Mazzini of course considered he owed none at all. This necessarily coloured all his actions, especially as to this sense of duty was added the profound conviction that the best condition for Italy was one of constitutional subjection to Victor Emmanuel. His constitutionalism was as much opportunist as the result of personal prejudice; he had the art of managing a chamber of deputies so well developed that he was rarely hampered by constitutional difficulties. As a constructive statesman there are few to compare with him; his achievements in the rebuilding of the Kingdom of Sardinia after the disasters of 1848-49 were amazingly prolific. The ten years between Novara and Magenta saw an immense increase in the wealth and prosperity of the kingdom. It was a result due almost entirely to his energy and foresight—he introduced Free Trade, it is true, but there is reason to believe that, under his energetic guidance, Piedmont would have been just as prosperous under a tariff system. As a life's work, this result of those ten years would have been one of which anyone could be proud; yet it was only a part, perhaps the smallest part, of what Cavour achieved. Six years after Sardinia had been beaten to the earth by Austria, he raised her to a position whence she could confer in equality with the Powers of Europe; he raised the condition of the subject peoples of Italy from an Italian question to a European one. Step by step he isolated Austria; step by step he won sympathy for Piedmont. He won from Napoleon III a grudging promise to help Victor Emmanuel in the event of an attack by Austria within a limited time; he saw to it that Austria made that attack within those time limits.

The one point on which there may not be unqualified approval of Cavour's policy is that of the cession of Savoy and Nice. It was a big sacrifice to make; of more importance was it that Italy did not achieve unity by her own exertions. Magenta and Solferino were French victories, beside which the glory of Palestro and San Martino paled into insignificance. Once the interference of France in Italian affairs was officially approved by Cavour, a precedent was afforded for the occupation of Rome and for constant French meddling in domestic policy.

Yet on the other hand there is much to be said

in favour of the sacrifice.   Italy without an ally had
not achieved independence in 1848, when all the
other conditions were in her favour.   She might
never succeed.   The Sardinian army was no match
for the Austrians in numbers, nor perhaps in
efficiency.   The other States of Italy had no force to
compare even with the Sardinians.   There was the
point to consider that if France were not admitted
into Italy as an ally she might one day force an
entrance as an enemy.   Lombardy and Venice, in
terms of population and wealth, were worth a dozen
of Savoy.   Cavour might even have thought that in
course of time an opportunity would come when Italy
would have a chance to free herself by her own
exertions—but that time might be far off, when there
would not be a Cavour or a Victor Emmanuel at the
head of Sardinian affairs.   He had laboured to make
the iron hot; he was determined to strike while it
remained hot.

Allied to his amused tolerance of constitutional
methods (undoubted constitutionalist though he was,
in his youth) was his active dislike of Mazzini, his aims
and his methods.   Republican rule meant anarchy
to his mind; revolts that were not aimed at annexation to Piedmont might as well, in his opinion, be
aimed against Piedmont.   He could never forget the
terrible difficulties in which he was placed by
Mazzini's rebellion in Genoa.   In consequence he
was opposed to any scheme in which he thought he
could discern Mazzini's handiwork; he was deeply
suspicious of and antagonistic to Garibaldi and Crispi
because they had once been Mazzini's men.   Because
of this there grew up the unfortunate schism between
Crispi and Cavour, and between Crispi and the
Cavour tradition, which became such an important
factor in Italian politics, and which nearly wrecked
Italy more than once.

On one occasion Cavour's political insight and
practical estimation of chances were sadly at fault.

That was when Napoleon III concluded, with Victor Emmanuel's agreement, the armistice of Villafranca. He was blinded by his disappointment, and the patience of ten years suddenly came to an end. It seems strange that he did not foresee the inevitable trend of events, nor how Napoleon's antagonism could be nullified by making dexterous play with "the will of the people." It was not long, however, before his opinion changed, and he came back to power to guide Italy through the troubles and stresses of the Congress of Zurich and the conquest of Naples.

His last achievement was the devising of a plan to reconcile Church and State—or at least to ensure their harmonious combined existence. He did not live to see the plan in action, but it was nevertheless the basis of all subsequent arrangements. And that by itself would be an ample monument to him.

His political achievements may be ranked with Garibaldi's feats of arms, and his record was unsmirched by any failure comparable to the latter's.

Above and beyond these three, developing their successes to the utmost, minimizing their failures, supporting them against all opposition when they were in the right, reining them back when they were set on taking the wrong path, encouraging and rewarding, was the man without whom all their efforts would have been doomed to failure. That was Victor Emmanuel.

In the Italian situation he filled the same function as the fly-wheel of an engine, reducing fluctuations to a minimum. In strict justice he is entitled to all the merit of Cavour's achievements, for without his help Cavour could have done nothing. The responsibility of failure would have been Victor Emmanuel's; he deserved the reward of success. On his accession to the throne, young, untried, depressed by an utter and irredeemable defeat, he nevertheless rose to the occasion in magnificent fashion—and Cavour was not his adviser then. He put aside the insidious Austrian offers with dignity and yet with tact. In his proclamation to his people he made certain promises, and he kept them all his life. Then he did Italy a great service by his selection of Cavour as head of the Cabinet. He saw that Cavour was the man for the situation, and he maintained him there through thick and thin. Besides Cavour he was almost the only man in Sardinia who saw the benefits to be derived from participation in the Crimean War. Had he not exerted all his influence Sardinia would never have participated—and might never have received Lombardy as indirect reward. It was a victory of strength of will and singleness of purpose. In the same way he forced through the military reforms which he and La Marmora considered advisable ; and the fruit of these reforms were the victories of Palestro, San Martino, and Castelfidardo. When Cavour failed him after Villafranca he assumed the burden of affairs—a heavy burden at that time—and dexterously out-manœuvred Pope and Emperor with a tact that Cavour could hardly have equalled. And when Cavour recovered from his fit of pettishness, he received him back into office, bearing no malice for his temporary desertion, knowing as he did that Cavour was still the best possible man for the post.

Like his unwavering support of Cavour was his complete belief in Garibaldi's integrity. Here again he demonstrated his ability to estimate character. Garibaldi had declared himself for " Italy and Victor Emmanuel," and the King knew him well enough to be sure that he would stand by his proclamation. He could not succeed, however, in quieting Cavour's fears on the subject.

From the time of the Crimea onwards, Victor Emmanuel enjoyed an enormous popularity, not only

I

in Italy, but all over Europe. " Il Re Galantuomo " was acclaimed everywhere. There were pictures of him in all the shops. His slight figure and his ferocious moustache were as well-known in England as were Gladstone's collars or Dickens' beard. It was a result almost entirely due to his magnificent honesty, honesty of purpose as well as of deed. Compared with what was remembered of Metternich, and compared with what was obvious about Napoleon III, Victor Emmanuel was an angel of light. His chivalrous policy was a relief after Louis Philippe's bourgeois cunning, and his courage, both physical and moral, as evinced at and after Novara, stood out prominently against the feebleness of the other Italian monarchs. He possessed all and more of King Bomba's furious energy with none of his savagery or periods of inertia. And to crown it all, he was haloed with success; the success of the rebuilding of the Kingdom of Sardinia; the success of Palestro, of San Martino, of Castelfidardo; he shared Garibaldi's glory; it is hardly surprising that his prestige was enormous. He used it with moderation and care. At any period in his reign after 1855 he could have made himself absolute. Yet he did not. His influence was frequently exerted, it is true, but always constitutionally and, as events proved, always to good purpose. He did not hesitate to pit his strength against Garibaldi's when it came to the parting of the ways, and time was to show that his restraint of Garibaldi was for the eventual good of Italy.

Had Mazzini, Garibaldi, and Cavour been weaker and less gifted men Italy might still have struggled forward to union and independence; without Victor Emmanuel it would have been impossible. But it must always be remembered that the greatest share in the freeing of Italy was borne by the men who revolted in Milan, by those who flung their lives away in Brescia, by those who gave their all to

finance Garibaldi, by the Bersaglieri who went
cheering to their deaths at San Martino; it was
a freedom bought at the price of thousands
and millions of unquestioning and unrecorded
sacrifices.

CHAPTER X

AN INCIDENT IN CALABRIA

ON the 18th of February, 1861, Victor Emmanuel opened the first Italian Parliament in Turin, and Italy, freed from the whims of individual tyrants, was delivered over to the whims of party. And party passion ran high, despite the fact that Cavour's skilful electioneering and the prestige of his success had established him with an overwhelming majority in the lower House.

There were several debatable points to be settled. The most pressing question was the recognition of Garibaldi's army. It would be an exceeding waste of good material to disband it, and furthermore, it was a little doubtful whether it would permit itself to be disbanded. Yet something had to be done. It was impossible that a private individual, even one of Garibaldi's standing, should be allowed to maintain a force of twenty thousand men in the State.

Yet there were powerful influences at work against the regularization of their position. The army objected strongly. It was jealous of, and prejudiced against the volunteers. Even Garibaldi was not popular with the Italian regulars. Sufficient time had not yet elapsed for the elimination of the old feudal traditions of the army, when none but men of noble birth could hold commissions, and the nobility still regarded the army as its own special preserve. But Victor Emmanuel came to Cavour's rescue as usual, and the measure was passed. Garibaldi's

132

regiments became Royal regiments; his lieutenant-generals became divisional and brigade commanders; only Garibaldi was omitted from the list, and that was at his own request. It was bad for the army, most probably; the men who followed Garibaldi were not of the type who take kindly to barrack life and routine business, but it was the best way out of the difficulty. Even as it was, it left a general soreness that militated against Cavour's popularity.

The next question was that of the position of the Church. Some working arrangement had to be devised. Different degrees of religious tolerance had been in evidence over the peninsula before the union. In Piedmont the reformed Church was allowed to exist, and no more. In Tuscany there had been enlightened freedom (in this one matter). In Naples heretics were officially not supposed to set foot, the Host and the Holy Oils were guarded by soldiers with fixed bayonets who compelled all passers-by to fall on their knees; the Catholic religion was sternly inculcated in the few schools, and only partakers of the Catholic communion were allowed to hold office. The settlement of these anomalies, and the establishment of a single practice throughout the country, called for moderation and for discretion, and neither was possible in a Parliament broken up into groups where parties increased inordinately the extravagance of their demands in order to retain the allegiance of the extremer groups. The matter was complicated by reason of the quarrel between the King and the Pope. Pius refused to recognize any of Victor Emmanuel's recent annexations; he persisted in addressing him as " King of Sardinia," and he would offer no help whatever in the reorganization of the Italian Church. He was a hindrance to the national progress; he endeavoured to thwart every one of the designs of Victor Emmanuel's government.

Just as some sort of settlement was arrived at in

the Parliament, thanks to the tact of the party in power, Cavour, to whom all the credit was due, died, worn out with his manifold exertions. It was a severe blow to Italy; there was no one else, not even Crispi, who could equal him in the ability to persuade, cajole, or coerce a distracted house of representatives. However, a working system had been devised, just in time. The government passed on to the questions of the Temporal Power, the relations with the other States of Europe, and the foreign policy to be adopted.

The significance of the wording of the title assumed by Victor Emmanuel should be noticed. He had been Victor Emmanuel II, by the Grace of God King of Sardinia; he now became Victor Emmanuel II, by the Grace of God and the Will of the People King of Italy. The numeral was important. As a rule potentates changing the style of the States they ruled changed their numeral too. Francis II, Holy Roman Emperor, became Francis I, Emperor of Austria. The last Duke of Savoy, Victor Amadeus II, became Victor Amadeus I, King of Sardinia. James VI of Scotland was James I of England. But Victor Emmanuel became Victor Emmanuel II of Italy, although there had never been a Victor Emmanuel, King of Italy, before. There were two possible explanations. One was that the Kings of Sardinia had always been legitimate Kings of Italy; the other that Italy became a part of Sardinia by conquest, as opposed to Sardinia being a part of Italy. To the theory of conquest the House of Savoy clung tenaciously; it was a useful justification for the enforcement of the Sardinian codes throughout Italy, but at the same time it was wounding to Neapolitan and Romagnol susceptibilities. Yet the House of Savoy had to make sacrifices as well. Savoy was gone from them; no longer could the heir to the throne bear the centuries-old title of Duke of Savoy. The title was

FRANCIS II
KING OF THE TWO SICILIES

not abandoned officially ; instead, it was merged into one higher in the scale.   Young Humbert, Duke of Savoy, became Prince of Naples, in an attempt to satisfy the injured Neapolitan *amour propre*.   It was an inevitable choice, for that matter, because Naples was now the largest town in the King of Italy's dominions.   The Royal family was now represented by the direct line (Victor Emmanuel and his only son, the Prince of Naples) by the House of Genoa, descended from Ferdinand, Victor Emmanuel's brother, and by that of Savoy-Carignan, a younger offshoot of the branch from which the King sprang, and promoted to the Duchy vacated by the accession of the then Duke, Charles Albert.   Care was taken that against Humbert could not be repeated the sneers which had been uttered in early days against Victor Emmanuel—that he had an Austrian wife and mother.   A marriage between Humbert and his cousin, daughter of Ferdinand of Genoa, was early arranged.   It had the advantage of not complicating foreign relations (they were complicated enough already) and of giving Italy an Italian princess for her future queen.   As Victor Emmanuel was half Austrian by blood, and Humbert three-quarters Austrian, there was need for this arrangement.

It was not long before Victor Emmanuel's title was generally recognized.   England acknowledged it at once; the German powers followed her example, and in the end Napoleon III reluctantly yielded to the inevitable, accredited a minister once more to Turin, and condescended to speak of " his brother of Italy."   The one ruler who refused to do so was the Pope—to him Victor Emmanuel remained King of Sardinia.

There were acute as well as chronic aspects to the Papal question.   Francis of Naples now lived in Rome, where he was treated with honour as a sovereign by Pius.   Pope and King combined to make Rome a thorn in the side of Italy.   Between

them they organized gangs of banditti, who
penetrated into the southern provinces, plundering
and destroying, assured of an asylum in the Papal
State as soon as the police and soldiers pressed them
too sharply to be comfortable. Here they were left
unharassed; in fact it is even said that they were
fêted and feasted, before being sent forth again with
a royal " Godspeed " and a Papal benediction. In
consequence of their depredations, of the plotting of
those Neapolitan nobles who had lost by the change
of masters, and of the general feeling of unrest,
Naples was kept in a ferment. Drastic, even
ferocious, measures failed to stamp out the evil—it
could obviously only be stamped out by the occupation of the Papal territory. The government was
driven to unstatesmanlike measures. Police officials
and ministers of state were compelled to enter into
negotiation with the secret societies, the Camorra and
the Mafia, and it was a fatal sign of weakness. It
was not very long before these societies had their
grip on the government services, and began to make
their influence felt in various underhand directions.
Between brigandage, independent, Royal and Papal,
and the struggles of the secret societies, the
condition of Sicily and Naples remained hardly
improved since the good old days of the Bourbons.

The one support of the Temporal Power was
France—or rather, Napoleon III. He needed the
support of the Church for his dynasty, and he used
every means in his power to retain it. A French
garrison occupied Rome on several occasions. He
was always ready to send men and to spend money
to help Pius, and he was ready, Victor Emmanuel
knew, to fight Italy on the question of the Temporal
Power. Victor Emmanuel realized that he was helpless against the power of France, although some of
his politicians would not have been averse to sending
Italy's half-formed armies against the foremost
military power in Europe. Cavour could do nothing.

Pius met his requests and suggestions with a weary
" *Non possumus* "; Napoleon III only answered
" *Jamais, jamais*," when the suggestion of the
Italian occupation of Rome was suggested. Cavour
died, and almost his last words expressed his ambition
—" *Libera chiesa in libero stato*."

The Papal retention of the Patrimony was
galling. More than one Italian came forward with
suggestions for the solution of the difficulty, but
suggestions were unavailing against the Papal " *Non
possumus*." Then came Garibaldi, the man who had
cut such knots before. Just at present his glory was
a little faded; he had tried to raise Venetia against
Austria, and his expedition had ended not only in
disaster, but in fantastic failure. Now he was determined to strike another blow for Italy, to redeem his
prestige—for his prestige was one of Italy's most
valuable assets. He had an interview with Victor
Emmanuel, though what took place there has never
been described and never will be. Garibaldi's actions
were watched with painful expectancy by all Italy;
they knew of his failure in Tyrol; they knew that he
had seen the King; then they saw him depart immediately for Sicily. There, at Palermo, he had interviews
with the Royal Princes—Umberto, Prince of Naples,
Thomas, Duke of Genoa, and the Duke of Savoy-
Carignan. From Palermo he went to Marsala—the
place sacred in Italian memory as the starting-point
of the expedition of the thousand. Italy watched
and waited—heard rumours of the gathering of the
old Garibaldists, of an oath taken in Marsala
Cathedral—" *Roma o morte*." There was a well-
accredited story of landings of arms with official
sanction. Then Garibaldi brought four thousand
men across the Straits of Messina and landed them
in Calabria. The rumour ran that the Royal troops,
hurriedly gathered to stop him, made way on reading
an official letter that he carried. But it did not
last long. More regiments barred his path at

Aspromonte, and this time they demanded his withdrawal and the disbandment of his army. Garibaldi refused. The regulars persisted. Garibaldi swore he would cut a path for himself. He led his men forward. They were repulsed with loss. Then Garibaldi fell, shot through the ankle, and his army broke up. He himself fell a prisoner into Italian hands. He might have been shot, but instead he was hurried away, given the best medical treatment, and packed off to his island home of Caprera.

What had happened cannot be known. The results were obvious. Garibaldi had acted in the belief, real or assumed, that he had the King's sanction. He considered himself betrayed by Victor Emmanuel, and all friendship between the two great men was at an end. Italy tried to draw her own conclusions, but could find no conclusion to draw. She could not believe Victor Emmanuel guilty of treachery; she could not believe Garibaldi foolish enough to misunderstand him. The ministry fell, the splendid majority that Cavour had left was shaken by defections from the Left and the extreme Right. The question of Rome was reduced to a party matter, although no party adhered to a determined policy of action save for the Republican Left.

Yet there can be surmises. Perhaps Garibaldi had offered his services to Victor Emmanuel; a similar expedition to the Sicilian one might have been arranged. The expedition would test European feeling. Victor Emmanuel may have found European feeling too strongly against the occupation of Rome; he must have sent orders to stop it, and found Garibaldi, once started, with the bit between his teeth, determined to see the matter through to the end. The cause of the dissension between the King and Garibaldi may have been that the latter thought the former too ready to bow to foreign intervention; he may (it is possible) have read into Victor Emmanuel's instructions to halt a private hint that the way would still be open to him on the display of a sufficient amount of force to justify Victor Emmanuel's giving way on the point. The battle might have arisen from too hasty action on the part of a subordinate, from an accidental shot fired, from any one of the myriad possible causes which may precipitate matters when armed forces are massed in opposition.

Probably the whole affair was the result of Napoleon III's desperate and underhand policy. Determined on bringing about dissension in Italy, he may have given Victor Emmanuel sufficient reason for believing that he would sanction an attempt on Rome, and then, when Garibaldi had once started, he may have demanded his recall on pain of war. Napoleon was fully capable of such a manœuvre. He stood to gain much. A violent civil war between Victor Emmanuel and Garibaldi, tearing Italy to pieces, and giving Pius an opportunity of reconquering Umbria and the Marches, would have delighted him—and it was within the bounds of possibility. And he had certainly taken precautions lest Garibaldi should slip past the armies sent to stop him. His fleet was off the Italian coast with orders to land sufficient men to hold Rome or to defeat the Redshirts. At the least, he had been given an opportunity to display his arbitrary will and his power to sway the policy of Europe. France's vanity, and his own, had been gratified, and he was afforded an opportunity to garrison Rome.

It was a brutal action, and one probably ill-judged. Napoleon seems to have over-estimated the influence of the Church over France; he cared, at that time, little for Italy's friendship, and he desired her to remain weak. Had he allowed Italy to take possession of Rome he would have gained by Italy's gratitude perhaps more than he would have lost by the change in the attitude of the Church—for the Church had no wish to make a desperate enemy of him. And he could have made an imperial gesture of his condescension in permitting Italy to occupy her rightful capital.

Garibaldi retired in disgust to Caprera; the Opposition rejoiced; Victor Emmanuel was bitterly disappointed; and Pius could still drive through the streets of Rome.

CHAPTER XI

UNITED ITALY

DISRUPTIVE influences were early apparent. Premier succeeded premier with the bewildering rapidity characteristic of Continental parliaments. There was no man left in Italy, save perhaps for the old Garibaldist Crispi, with the skill and force of character to steer the Parliament through the continual crises which developed, and Crispi was still under a cloud through his connection with Garibaldi and the affair of Aspromonte. Rattazzi had followed Cavour, Farini followed Rattazzi, Minghetti followed Farini. None of them was of any avail. "Any fool can govern by proclaiming a state of siege," had said Cavour, and while he lived states of siege and martial law were avoided. But after his death martial law was reintroduced; a state of siege was proclaimed in the southern provinces, and the soldiers of Piedmont were let loose on unhappy Naples in an endeavour —vain as regards the societies—to restrain the banditti and the secret societies.

Cialdini was military governor; he was the man who had won the victory of Castelfidardo. He found his hands full. The banditti had the solid support of Ferdinand of Naples, and the open countenance of Pius, while any action of his was called to account with gusto by a violent and malicious opposition at Turin. When Manhes had put down Calabria during the reign of Murat he had been uncompromisingly backed not only by his sovereign, but by the whole

141

might of the French Empire—little matters like hangings and quarterings, and faintly illegal legal processes like torture, found no mention in the press, and there was no opposition to exaggerate or even to tell the truth.

Feeble violence is worse than useless when employed to pacify a state in smouldering insurrection, and Cialdini could employ no other kind. The opposition would be worthy of praise if they had only condemned his actions because they did not approve of them; but it is only too obvious that the deputies merely considered them in the light of a party matter, for when the government fell, as was almost immediately inevitable, the new party in power continued the same methods, and sustained Cialdini in the command, while the defeated party promptly threw itself into the business of condemning actions similar to those which they had ordered only a month or two ago. In fact, there appears to be a decided superficial similarity between the Neapolitan and the Irish questions.

Napoleon continued his meddling with Italian affairs. In no way averse to seeing dissension in Italy, he was darkly suspected of aiding the rebels almost to the same extent as Ferdinand, while he posed to France and Europe as the friend of the Papacy and sought to find some definite practicable arrangement for the conservation of the Papal power. At length it seemed as if he succeeded.

The presence of a French garrison in Rome was galling to the Italians. To ensure its removal the Italians were prepared to make considerable sacrifices, and these sacrifices were exacted to the full. In exchange for the withdrawal of the French Victor Emmanuel promised to guarantee the Papal State against all other Powers; to agree to the raising of a Papal army; and to transfer his capital from Turin to Florence.

It is difficult to appreciate the effect of these

stipulations. A similar state of affairs might have
arisen in England if, on the accession of James I
to the throne of Great Britain, Henri IV of France
had maintained the Archbishop of Canterbury as an
absolute King of London, and had compelled James
to transfer his capital from Edinburgh to Lancaster
or Pembroke. Such an arrangement would have
been hardly less absurd than the Convention of
September.

It would not have mattered so much had Pius
been a popular monarch in Rome, but he was not.
Like one of Mr. Wells' mechanics, who had read
Shakespeare, and found him weak in chemistry, the
Roman people had suffered under Pius and found
him weak in political science. Rome was abominably
badly governed; corruption and maladministration of
justice flourished just as they had done in the good
old days before 1848. The only reason that a small
party favourable to Pius could put forward in his
favour, was that his presence in Rome brought a
certain number of rich travellers to the city, who
spent a certain amount of money there, and this
argument made only a small appeal to the people.
They were anxious to see Rome part of Italy—it was
only the inertia resulting from centuries of appalling
conditions which kept them quiet at all.

Nevertheless, Victor Emmanuel had to agree; the
French troops were withdrawn, and Pius continued
to maintain himself on his uneasy throne by the aid
of his Swiss and German mercenaries.

The transference of the capital meant trouble.
Turin, the residence of the princes of the House of
Savoy for five hundred years, almost rose in rebellion
when the Convention was made public. In the
north, as in the south, martial law had to be
proclaimed. The troops had to disperse rioters,
firing on the mobs. The little milliners of the town
realized woefully that no longer would there be
befeathered Bersaglieri in garrison in the town for

them to walk with through Valentino park; the shopkeepers realized that no longer would the Court and the hundreds of deputies be present in the town to spend their annual millions. It was a serious blow to the prosperity of Turin. Napoleon might well be pleased with the result of his meddling. Southern Italy was already in a ferment; now, he thought, the north, the foundation of Victor Emmanuel's power, would also be antagonized. To Napoleon's account must be laid the blood that was shed in the streets of Turin in October, 1864. His subtle manœuvring had deprived Victor Emmanuel of the support—of the wholehearted support, at least—of both the Left and the Right, of Garibaldi and of the Piedmontese nobility. He could apparently congratulate himself; an Italy united in name and divided in fact was all that he desired to enable him to pose as the champion of the popular idea, and at the same time obviate any possible danger to France arising from a powerful neighbour on her south-eastern frontier.

It is perfectly possible that this plan of dividing Italy was only secondary to the main idea of gratifying France's vanity and his own by a display of arbitrary power. It is significant that the French Minister at Turin was Benedetti. A name of ill omen this. Only six years later M. Benedetti was to be the French Minister to Prussia; forced on by the urgent orders of Grammont and others, he was to inflict his presence on King William, holiday-making at Ems, and to clamour for a definite guarantee that the withdrawal of the Hohenzollern candidature for the Spanish throne would be permanent; and Bismarck's version of his reception was to be the starting-point of the war that was to pull Napoleon III from the throne of his uncle. Napoleon was certainly seeking no more than a diplomatic victory then; very possibly he sought no more now. It was so that he might boast of a petty and unfruitful wordy success that the excitable Torinese mechanics died in Turin streets.

However it was, it is undoubted that Napoleon's success was only to be transient. On the face of it, the friendship of Italy was worth more to him than any paper victory. Moreover, he assumed that the transfer of the Italian capital would imply that the seat of government was to remain permanently in Florence—but the rest of Europe sprang to the conclusion that Florence was only a half-way house towards Rome. Above all, he underestimated Victor Emmanuel. The King was the mightiest man in Italy; his word swayed at least one half of the country, and he was always careful to ensure that the other half was not all in direct opposition to him. The affair of Aspromonte had damaged Garibaldi's prestige far more than it had Victor Emmanuel's, which was no bad thing in its way, for Garibaldi previously had been far too powerful for the good of the State, however pure his motives and disinterested his ambitions. The chaos of parties in Parliament involved little more than a certain continual friction and clumsiness in the executive as long as Victor Emmanuel lived—in itself it signified nothing. It was merely the inevitable concomitant of party government as practised by nations unaccustomed to, and hardly fitted for, the innovation.

The King's word was law in fact if not in theory; it was his influence, brought powerfully to bear, which ensured to a large extent the maintenance of the policy of Cavour. The commercial development of the country was pushed on apace. The Mont Cenis tunnel was by this time finished; the great (State) railway through Emilia to Ancona, and thence eventually to Naples and to Brindisi, was laid down in an incredibly short time. If an object lesson were ever needed to demonstrate the blessings of unity to the Italian people, this supplied it. And with the railways and the making of practicable

K

roads the brigandage of the Neapolitan provinces could at last be suppressed.

La Marmora was by this time first Minister of State. His predecessor had not been able to retain his power after the conclusion of the convention of September, 1864. Apart from Crispi, La Marmora was the man for the position. Enormous force of character was needed; in place of Cavour's dexterous handling of political parties La Marmora employed, almost equally successfully, a brute force method of passing unpopular measures through Parliament. He governed the House of Representatives with military discipline, and it was well he did so, for the disruptive elements had become unduly noisy, if not powerful. Taxation was enormous; it seemed beyond the power of any finance minister to balance his budgets. For a time the railways were distinctly unprofitable, yet more money was continually being spent on extending them. The collection of the revenue was still inefficient, the officials charged with the duty were still under the influence of the traditions of the old régime, and the disturbed state of the south militated powerfully against the development of a good civil service.

But money had to be raised. Bearing in mind the opportunist nature of Napoleon's foreign policy and his uncompromising attitude with regard to Rome, war with France was always a distinct possibility. That meant that there had to be an Italian fleet to guard the Italian coasts and the Italian islands. Thanks to Napoleon, too, the Quadrilateral was still in Austrian hands. The Austro-Italian frontier was almost impregnable to the Italians in consequence, while nothing would be easier than an Austrian invasion of Italy. A surprise attack was possible, if not probable, and it might be fatal. A huge Italian army had to be maintained almost on a war footing to guard against it. It was not a cheap army. Garibaldi's volunteers, lately incorporated, might be intensely patriotic, but they were vastly expensive. The semi-voluntary method of recruiting cost a great deal of money. And, inevitably, the money was not employed to the best advantage—it was the civil service that disbursed it. Peculation, corruption, nepotism and bribery; the Italy for which nameless heroes without number had poured out their blood for fifty years was caught in their toils. La Marmora and Victor Emmanuel did their best, and their best was much, but the handicaps under which they laboured were too heavy.

Somehow things were done, although the public credit reeled unstably. There were three hundred thousand men in the active army, and the fleet was the fourth most powerful in the world. Italy was nearly ready (as ready as she ever would be, said the pessimists) to take yet another stride towards completion and towards a place among the Powers of Europe. Something was bound to happen shortly, and events which had taken place on the other side of Europe seemed to indicate to the meanest intelligence the scene of the new development.

CHAPTER XII

VENICE

SINCE 1859 the Austrian treatment of Venetia had altered in many ways for the better; in some, if possible, for the worse. Francis Joseph had come to realize that a dissatisfied province was more of a liability than an asset (Hungary had shown him that, as well as Lombardy), and he had done his best in his unenlightened and conscientious way to lessen some of the burdens of the unhappy province. He had granted a very limited form of self-government; he had impressed upon his white-coated troops the need for respecting national prejudices to a certain extent; he had tried to exploit his own growing personal popularity.

It was of no avail. The Venetians remained stiff-necked in their intolerance of the Austrian yoke. They had too splendid a national history of their own to submit tamely to the rule of the barbarian. The nation which had set up and pulled down Roman Emperors, in the days when the Hapsburgs were petty feudal noblemen, was hardly likely to be impressed by the splendour of Austrian royalty; the memory of Manin, "the last of the Doges," was still green. For a whole year, not two decades ago, Venice had defied all the might of the Empire, and what Venetians had done Venetians might still do. And Manin, the latest of the Venetian heroes, had, before his death, declared for Italy and Victor Emmanuel. His dying words bore weight. Nothing

148

short of annexation to Italy would satisfy the
Venetians, and they turned with contempt from
Austrian efforts at reconciliation and compromise.

Francis Joseph found their contempt galling.
Once one of his Viceroys had, during a State visit,
found the palaces of the Grand Canal placarded with
bills wishing long life to Verdi—"*Viva Verdi.*"
Nothing very harmful about paying compliments to
a rising young musician perhaps, but " Verdi " was
also the initials of Victor Emmanuel Re d'Italia. It
was exasperating and annoying, but Francis Joseph
continued his blundering attempts at reconciliation,
although he kept the place filled with troops—Czechs
and Hungarians—at the same time as he conscripted
the Venetian youth and sent his Italian regiments
to hold down Bohemia and Hungary.

There was much more to worry him than the
questions of Venice and Hungary. His dominion
over Germany was being challenged. When
Francis I had abandoned his title of Holy Roman
Emperor in favour of that of Hereditary Emperor
of Austria, he had not pretended to give up his ill-
defined claims on the overlordship of the German
Empire. In abeyance during the Napoleon era, they
had nevertheless been tacitly admitted in 1815. The
South German States followed Austria's lead in most
points of policy, and Prussia, the most powerful
state of North Germany, grudgingly yielded her
precedence as well. Yet Prussia was not at all
satisfied, and worked steadily towards the destruction
of Austrian influence in Germany. For a space she
was successful; she contrived matters so that the
lesser North German States joined her in a customs
union—Zollverein—while Austria stood disdainfully
aloof. In consequence the bonds between Prussia
and her small neighbours were drawn closer. Then
came the memorable year of 1848, when thrones
were tottering all over Europe.

Yet in Germany the agitation had the curious

result of an attempt to set up yet another throne,
for the Germans, anxious to form a closer union,
decided on a German Empire, and offered the
Imperial crown to the King of Prussia. It was
declined. No Hohenzollern would accept a crown
from a popular party; that would be too undignified
and constitutional—besides, what a committee might
give a committee might take away. Nevertheless,
the incident proved that Prussia was drawing near
to her ambition of dominating all Germany. Austria
realized that it was time for her to assert herself.
The opportunity came almost at once. Hesse,
abominably misgoverned, rose in revolt the next
year. Prussian troops entered Hessian territory to
end the troubles the Prussian way, and found
Austrian troops already there, called in by the other
members of the Bund. Prussians and Austrians
glared at each other across the body of prostrate
Hesse. Austria was flushed with the victories
recently gained at the expense of unfortunate Charles
Albert. Strong in the memory of Custozza and
Novara, reassured as to Hungary by the promised
help of Russia, Austria declared that she was
prepared to enforce her wishes by war. Prussian
troops had not been in action since Waterloo; the
rest of the Bund was undoubtedly opposed to her;
grave defects were already obvious in the Prussian
mobilization system and in the military organization,
and in the end the King of Prussia flinched. He
gave way on every point, and humbled himself to
the triumphant Austrians. The infant Bund, and
Prussia's six months old overlordship of Germany,
perished simultaneously. Austria was once more
supreme in Germany.

The lesson was accentuated by the little war that
developed the next year between Prussia and
Denmark. Prussia had no navy, and the Danes
fought with their accustomed bravery. Sea power
and dogged courage won the day for the Danes, and

the hour of reckoning was postponed.   Once more Prussia gave way.

From 1850 onwards, Prussia had been taking steps in her deliberate German fashion to ensure that never again would she be so humiliated and defeated. A young diplomat, Bismarck, saw to it that she was not embroiled prematurely again before she was reorganized. He bullied the Reichstag into granting the necessary money to enable reforms to be carried out, and when the Reichstag turned obstinate he devised a series of expedients whereby the Reichstag's obstinacy was made unavailing. A trio of remarkable men, King William of Prussia, von Moltke, and von Roon, began to rebuild the army and to wipe out defects which had developed during forty years of peace. An opportune mobilization on the Rhine had the effect of bringing to light some additional flaws in the arrangements, and also brought Napoleon III's triumphant career in Italy to a sudden close. Prussia climbed slowly into the position of the foremost military power in Europe, although none yet realized the fact, apart from the men at the head of the Prussian army.

In 1864 came the death of the King of Denmark, the last of his line. In two of his provinces, Slesvig and Holstein, the succession was disputed, and these two provinces were members (or were alleged to be members) of the German Bund. Their fate was a matter of interest to all Germany. The lesser German kingdoms, Saxony and Hanover, in particular, at once began to take steps as to their future. Neither Prussia nor Austria could tolerate such independence. Saxony and Hanover were abruptly told to mind their own businesses and to leave such matters to the consideration of their betters. A combined Prussian and Austrian army poured into Slesvig and Holstein. The Danes fought well once more, but by this time there was some sort of Prussian navy in existence, the opposing forces were overwhelming, and European opinion on the subject was divided. Some of the Powers sincerely believed that the allies had right on their side; Napoleon III hesitated; England did nothing. Two or three dashing exploits by the Prussian army carried the invaders over arms of the sea which fourteen years ago had proved much more difficult obstacles. In the end Denmark gave way and ceded Slesvig and Holstein, of which Prussia and Austria remained in joint occupation. Bismarck had put into practice for the first time his dictum that it is blood and iron which welds an Empire together, and he had incidentally made the war of 1914-18 possible by putting the site of the future Kiel canal in Prussian hands.

The clumsy joint occupation was sure to end in trouble. That was obvious to all Europe. Sooner or later the allied plunderers would be sure to fall out over the ill-gotten gains, and the kingdoms of Germany began covertly furbishing up their weapons, and anxiously debating as to which side was the more likely to win.

Opinion was hardly divided. Saxony, Bavaria, and Hanover and Hesse-Cassel were positive that Austria was bound to be victorious, and entered into alliance with the Empire, their mouths watering at the prospect of fat pickings later in Rhenish Prussia and Prussian Saxony and the North Sea littoral. Napoleon III inclined to the same opinion, but he thought that it would be a long and exhausting war, at the end of which he could step in with his fresh army and secure for himself the position of arbiter of Germany, along with a few unconsidered trifles like Luxembourg or Belgium.

Outside of Prussia there were few men who thought that Prussia had the slightest chance of victory, but one of those few was the King of Italy. He had a high opinion of von Moltke, and he guessed shrewdly at what the Prussian army was capable of doing. The *zundnadel* had not been given a fair chance against the Danes, or, if it had, the critics had not read the lesson aright. He realized that the South German States would be at a disadvantage when opposed to a vigorous advance by the Prussian army, and that with its rapid mobilization the latter would be able to discount any disadvantage under which it might labour as regards numbers. Victor Emmanuel decided to back Prussia against Austria, knowing as he did so that the stake he was risking was his throne and his fame. The lessons learned at Custozza, Novara, at Magenta and San Martino, were now of service to him. It was a purely military point that had to be decided. There was no question of ethics. The Austrian treatment of Italy throughout the century justified Italy in striking back at any suitable moment. In Victor Emmanuel's opinion the present moment was suitable.

In March, 1866, the diplomatic world was mildly surprised by the arrival of a certain General Govone at Berlin. The explanation was put forward that he had come to study the Prussian military organization. Such an explanation might have been satisfactory in a time of profound peace, but at a time when all Europe was arming for a struggle obviously only a few months distant a different one was at once sought, and was found by some—shrewd guesses were made that he had come to arrange joint military action against Austria.

Napoleon III was seriously alarmed. Italy, the young nation for whose creation he took all the credit in the eyes of his Empire, was getting out of hand. It was not at all right that she should begin to win territory for herself; it should come only as a favour from him. Besides, Italy might turn the balance in favour of Prussia, and he had enough political foresight to realize that a strong Prussia was far more dangerous to him than a strong Austria. He hurriedly began diplomatic interference. As it happened, diplomacy was the only weapon ready to his hand.

Some years before he had found employment for his army in Mexico, where he had taken advantage of various sins of omission and commission on the part of the Mexicans to set up Francis Joseph's brother Maximilian (the same who had been Viceroy of Lombardo-Venetia during 1859) as Emperor of Mexico, and the best of the French Imperial army was at present fully occupied in maintaining Maximilian on his uneasy throne. War at the moment would be a serious inconvenience to him— and Victor Emmanuel was acutely aware of the fact. He was aware, too, that the United States, just emerging triumphantly from her Civil War, with an army of nearly a million veterans, would not long tolerate Napoleon's violation of the Monroe Doctrine. Napoleon would have to recall his troops, and then would be a far more dangerous arbitrator. The business had to be carried through at once.

Napoleon spoilt, by his flagrant self-seeking, his chances of composing the German differences. He hankered too obviously after " compensation " on the Rhine, and Austria was driven to protest against his interference in German affairs. He was smartly rebuffed; Italy paid no heed to his protests, and in April, 1866, concluded with Prussia a treaty of alliance, whereby she was assured that in the event of victory she would have Venetia for certain, and as much of the Trentino and Italian Tyrol as she could grab, and whose cession the military situation would warrant.

Some hint of the arrangement came through to Austria, and Francis Joseph, grown by now a little doubtful in the face of the determination of Prussia not to yield an inch, endeavoured to placate Italy and guard against an attack in rear. He offered to cede Venetia at once, without question.

It was a tempting offer. Victor Emmanuel was

in considerable doubt as to whether the tottering
finances of his kingdom could support the added
strain of war; he was doubtful of the efficiency of
his improvised army, formed largely as it was of
Garibaldist volunteers and ex-Neapolitan regulars.
There was another doubt, too. Prussia might be
beaten in the approaching campaign, and with
Prussia beaten the whole weight of Austria would
be brought to bear against Italy, and in that event,
with Austria holding the Quadrilateral with all its
attendant strategic advantages, there could be no
doubt at all as to the issue. The only doubt would
be as to the extent of the demands Austria would
make subsequently. Victor Emmanuel would have
to follow the example of his father and abdicate on
the field of another and greater Novara, and it was
even possible that his cherished Italy would be once
more broken up, and the hated Bourbon reset on the
throne of the Two Sicilies.

Yet there were cogent arguments on the other
side. First and foremost, Victor Emmanuel had
pledged his word to the Prussian alliance, and with
Victor Emmanuel, in contradistinction to other
European monarchs, his word was considered a
binding pledge. He had earned the name of the
Re Galantuomo, and he would not, not even for his
crown, bring a slur upon that name. There was also
the important point that, other things being equal,
honesty was undoubtedly the best policy. This was
the first international agreement into which Italy
had ever entered—it would be a bad start if it were
also the first to be broken. The terms of the alliance
distinctly stated that neither of the contracting parties
was to make peace without the consent of the other,
and the matter under present discussion certainly
seemed to be included in this clause. Besides—there
was always the chance that success would bring Italy
more than the province of Venetia which Francis
Joseph offered. Last of all came the consideration

that Italy was in a condition in which war would be a blessing. She was flabby and incoherent still—a period of severe strain and of a common cause would do much to unite the still nearly separate members. Victor Emmanuel pinned his faith to the *zundnadel*, to von Moltke, and to his own armies, rejected Francis Joseph's offer, and held firm to the Prussian alliance.

Bismarck meanwhile was working energetically and dexterously to take advantage of events as they occurred—with profound humility he made no claim to control them at all—to such good purpose that he speedily manoeuvred Austria into a position similar to that in which she had found herself on the eve of the campaign of Magenta. Bismarck could pose as the injured party, and could enlist the sympathy of that part of Europe not directly interested—of England and Russia mainly. Napoleon was only a helpless onlooker; England could do no harm in a short war; and Russia's friendship was assured. Bismarck industriously fanned the embers of dissension, and at once the flame of war broke forth. Victor Emmanuel issued a stirring call to his people, and dispatched his regiments on their mission to free Venetia.

Yet the paralysing hand of party politics and of international intrigue fell heavy on the Italian military arrangements. The divisional generals largely held their appointments by virtue of the support of various parliamentary parties, and were pledged to endeavour to carry out in the field the wishes of those parties. Napoleon III, frantic with rage at this determined and unsanctioned effort on the part of Italy, brought all the secret pressure to bear of which he was capable—and that was a great deal. Privately, through diplomatic channels, he impressed upon the Italian government that it might be well for Italy not to press Austria too hard and compel French intervention, while secretly he let it be known throughout the Italian government that the man who counselled moderation would be regarded with favour by the Emperor of the French. The device was successful. Napoleon had large resources at his command. Perhaps a little French gold trickled over the Alps; perhaps his mere veiled threat had effect; however it was, the ambitious and vigorous offensive campaign that Victor Emmanuel and La Marmora had planned was abandoned, apparently without the King's authority, and the Italian army was sent forward with improvised instructions and the absurd orders not to beat Austria too severely.

Yet war with Austria was the most popular policy that could be suggested to Italy. The mass of the people was wild with delight. Volunteers came forward in thousands to swell the ranks of the army —although it seems probable that this was a doubtful advantage, seeing that the recruits were largely enrolled, untrained, in the regular battalions and sent forward to the scene of action. Garibaldi once more took the field. He hurried to the scene of his earlier *fiasco*, the foothills of the Alps, with a few volunteers —his best men were now regulars of the Italian army—and tried to raise the populace there. He was not very successful, from a variety of causes.

La Marmora, the victor of the Tchernaya, the pacificator of Genoa and of Naples, resigned his premiership to take over the command in chief of the army of the Mincio. Cialdini, the hero of Palestro and of Castelfidardo, commanded the army of Romagna, and each of these men had under their command a hundred thousand troops. Seeing that they were separated the one from the other by the Quadrilateral, and that the whole success of the campaign depended upon their close co-operation, it would have been as well to have employed any two other men instead, for La Marmora and Cialdini were bitter political enemies, and had each the utmost contempt for the other's capacity. Cialdini could plead his instructions from the Ministry of War against any violent offensive action, and he hung back and let La Marmora dash himself against the Quadrilateral unsupported.

La Marmora brought his men successfully across the Mincio. One of his divisions was commanded by Humbert, the heir to the throne; one of his brigades was commanded by the heir's brother, Amadeus Duke of Aosta, later destined to occupy for a brief space the uneasy throne of Spain. The House of Savoy was to sustain in this campaign its ages-old military reputation.

Opposed to La Marmora was a redoubtable fraction of the Austrian army under a redoubtable leader. Benedek, the Austrian who had held San Martino so firmly against the Piedmontese on the day of Solferino, was now in Bohemia, contending at the head of a quarter of a million men against von Moltke, but the Archduke Albert was the best of his lieutenants. He was the son of the Archduke Charles, one of the few generals who could boast a victory over the great Napoleon, and he was no mean soldier, as the event was to prove. He had eighty thousand men and a strong position—enough to make La Marmora walk warily.

The latter did almost as much as could be expected of him. He crossed, as has been said, the Mincio without losing a man, and moved tentatively forward into the Quadrilateral. Peschiera and Mantua worried him, and he was compelled to send strong detachments to watch these two fortresses. Consequently he could only oppose equal forces to the Austrians when Albert flung himself, with every man he could collect, against the Italian position, which was situated, ominously enough, on those very heights of Custozza from which Charles Albert had been flung so disastrously eighteen years before.

All day long the Austrians dashed themselves

NAPOLEON III

against the Italian lines. At the very outset the day was nearly lost for Italy, and the battle was only stabilized by the opportune arrival of more troops from across the Mincio. Humbert headed his division with reckless valour; Amadeus was wounded and carried from the field. On the right Humbert was successful, and the Austrians were flung back in disorder; on the left Durando and Pianell held their ground after the first collision. Yet it was in the centre that the battle was to be lost and won. Here Govone—the same general who had negotiated the Prussian alliance—was in command, and he beheld with dismay a gradual massing of enemy brigades, largely drawn from the wings, in his front. Humbert, Govone, Durando, all sent pressing messages to La Marmora imploring him to strengthen his centre, even, if need be, at the expense of Humbert's victorious wing, but La Marmora disagreed. He feared lest it was only a feint on the part of Albert, and he distrusted the ability of the Italian army to move in order from one part of the battlefield to another. Unhandy troops and a general without vision! It might almost have been Novara over again.

The battle had been in progress for ten hours when Albert called upon his men for a supreme effort, and the white-coated Croats and Czechs responded gallantly enough. Struggling forward with magnificent self-devotion, they gained the summits of Monte Croce and Monte Belvedere, and finally, with one last effort of their failing strength, they captured the village of Custozza itself, the key of the Italian position.

The battle was lost for Italy. Happily night covered La Marmora's retreat, and he was able to extricate his dispirited divisions and fall back in some sort of order to the Mincio—and beyond. Venetia was still in Austrian hands. The news of the defeat paralysed Garibaldi's efforts in Tyrol; his feeble force of barely two thousand men could accomplish nothing in the face of Tyrolese apathy and a determined local resistance.

In Florence there was something like panic. Everyone feared lest the next news to arrive would be that Albert had dashed forward, making Napoleonic use of interior lines, and had struck down Cialdini as he had struck down La Marmora. Fortunately nothing like this occurred, although one can hardly help believing that a Napoleon at the head of the Austrian army would have been in Florence within a fortnight. Albert, like the Italian generals, was hampered by restraining orders from the capital, and his army had been even harder hit than had La Marmora's. A tenth of his men had fallen, and his force was for the moment too crippled to move.

After ten days of breathless suspense, the telegraph brought welcome news to Florence. Von Moltke had been successful in the very operation in which the Italians had failed, and which he, incidentally, described as the most difficult operation of war—the bringing of two separate armies simultaneously upon the same field of battle. Frederick and Frederick Charles of Prussia had come together on the field of Sadowa, caught Benedek between them, and the *zundnadel* had done the rest. Forty thousand Austrians had fallen, and the triumphant Prussians were now swarming forward against Vienna. On other battlefields they had done equally well; despite a bloody reverse at Langensalza, they had surrounded the Hanoverian army and compelled its surrender, and the South German troops had been similarly dealt with. At that very moment the furious Prussian hussars were riding down and sabring without mercy a few Austrian troops who had been dispatched to the assistance of the Bavarians—white-coated Austrians who died bravely but hopelessly. They were Italians—the conscripts from that very Venetia this war was to set free.

The day after Sadowa, Francis Joseph recalled Albert's victorious army to help in the defence of Vienna, and, seeing at the same time the hopelessness of trying to maintain his grasp upon Venetia, he appealed for Napoleon's intervention. To Napoleon he ceded Venetia, hoping in this way to keep the Italians out of the remainder of his dominions, and also, perhaps, hoping that the gift would stir up trouble between Italy and France.

Napoleon was delighted. Once more he could pose as the arbiter of Europe, and at the same time he could restrain the Italian attacks upon Austria. He accepted Venetia temporarily, at the same time as he accepted the invitation to mediate. He at once addressed himself to the Kings of Prussia and Italy. Prussia, under the guidance of Bismarck, bluntly told him to mind his own business; Italy referred him to Prussia, whose answer had already arrived.

Italy could not in honour accept Napoleon's offer of Venetia as the reward of immediate peace. She was irritated by Napoleon's continual meddling, and she could certainly not abandon her ally in the midst of the campaign. Besides, the national *amour propre* had been badly injured by the defeat of Custozza. La Marmora, to his eternal honour, consented to serve under Cialdini, a junior general and his hated enemy, and the united army pressed forward into Venetia, with never a " with your leave " or a " by your leave " to Napoleon.

The fortresses of the Quadrilateral were masked, and the Italians poured forth into Venetia. Garibaldi, with furious energy, made further desperate efforts to raise Tyrol. All Italy clamoured for a victory, for some substantial success worthy to rank with the old battle honours of the regiments —with Borodino and Solferino.

The press began to ask what had the navy done —the fourth most powerful in the world—for which the wretched lazzaroni had paid so dearly by grist

L

tax and poll tax. There was little that the navy
could do against the iron-bound Austrian coast, but
politicians with their minds on the next elections sent
for the order that something must be done.

The finest navy in the world is useless with a fool
in command, and the Italian admiral commanding
was worse than a fool. His record was good. He
had served all his life in the Sardinian navy, and
he was the first admiral to be appointed to the navy
of Italy. He had done good work as far as conditions
allowed during the Crimean War. But Persano must
have degenerated since those days, though none knew
it as yet. The situation called for the unflinching
courage of a Drake or a Farragut, and Persano was
in no way on the same plane as these. The con-
flicting orders he received, thanks to the complicated
political situation, might have deprived a bolder man
of his initiative. Failure, of course, meant his
professional ruin, but, apparently, an overwhelming
success would bring upon him the wrath of the
government to an equal extent. To send a weak-
nerved man to attack powerful fortifications with a
fleet only slightly superior to the enemy's, and yet to
tie him down to ridiculously small objectives, was to
court disaster.

Persano led the fleet up the Adriatic, looking
anxiously for some opening for a small yet decisive
success, hardly conscious as yet of the Diogenean
nature of his search. In the end he pitched upon
the island of Lissa as perhaps the nearest to his ideal.
He brought the fleet into action, ranging up and
down in front of the forts with which the island was
guarded, firing heavily with his smooth bore and
rifled guns against the concealed batteries. Once
more it was demonstrated that it is a risky matter
to pit ships against guns of position. The forts
returned the fire stoutly, and after many hours' firing
the Italians had made no progress and had received
some considerable damage. Persano withdrew to

effect repairs; he dared not return to port with nothing gained, so the repairs were executed in the open sea.

Meanwhile the Austrians had determined to strike back. They put the business in the hands of the best man for the purpose they could possibly have found—Tegetthoff, the man who had foiled the Danish fleet in 1864, and who was to build up a great reputation in Polar exploration. Every ship and man available was collected; like Farragut, Tegetthoff cared little about the iron on the ships as long as there was plenty of iron in the men. With a strange assortment of vessels—one or two modern ironclads, a few converted wooden ships, and even some old three-deckers adapted for steam—he came dashing out of harbour on the night of July 19. He caught the Italian fleet hardly prepared for the encounter. A fleet action was the last thing Persano had been expecting.

Persano got his fleet into battle formation, but the weakness of his nerve was immediately apparent. The most powerful of his units was the new " ram " *Affondatore*—" The Sinker "—and, just as the action began, he transferred his flag to her. The *Affondatore* was not intended to fight in the line; the fleet tactics required that she should lie outside it to snap up opportunities for ramming as they appeared, and it was for this reason originally that Persano had flown his flag in the *Re d'Italia*. However, at the last moment Persano had changed his mind, without informing the rest of the fleet, so that in the battle that developed captains looked in vain for signals from the *Re d'Italia*. Tegetthoff deliberately adopted tactics which might have been fatal against any other commander—he allowed Persano's line to " cross his T," forming a heavy column with his ships and rushing in berserk fashion straight at the centre of the Italian line. The Italians, observing no signals from the admiral, received the charge instead of keeping away, as their superior speed would easily have allowed, and blasting the Austrian ships to pieces with their superior artillery. The fleets were soon wrapped in smoke and badly tangled (black powder was still used), and Tegetthoff, the man of iron, went raging through the confusion looking for something to ram. The *Re di Portogallo* received his first attentions, escaped fatal damage from his ram, and nearly tore his ship to pieces with a broadside at five yards' range. Tegetthoff, not a bit discomposed, plunged on through the smoke, found the *Re d'Italia* with her steering gear put out of action by a shell, and sent the bows of the *Ferdinand Max* crashing into her side. She sank in two or three seconds with every soul on board. Almost at the same time another Italian ship, the *Palestro*, met the same fate as did the British battle-cruisers at Jutland—a stray shell reached her magazine and she blew up.

That decided the battle. Two appalling disasters and hours of helpless confusion broke the nerve of the Italian captains; the Austrians had received considerable damage from gunfire and were in no fit state to continue the battle. Tegetthoff had struck his blow for the honour of Austria, and without risking any more he turned his fleet back to Pola, while Persano retired to Ancona.

It was a staggering blow for Italy. There were riots in Florence as soon as the news was made public. Persano was put under arrest, and no sooner was that done than the *Affondatore*, caught in a sudden squall, turned turtle (after the engaging manner of turret ships all the world over) and sank with most of her crew. It would have been as well for Persano had he been still on board.

Francis Joseph was now ready to yield to the Prussians, who had advanced nearly to Vienna, and with a ruined fleet and a beaten army it was hopeless for Italy to try to continue the war by herself. Her

loss of naval strength, too, compelled Italy to listen
to the remonstrances of Napoleon III again, for,
even if Napoleon's best army was still in Mexico,
he had a fleet which, if England agreed, could
dominate the Mediterranean. Reluctantly Victor
Emmanuel agreed to an armistice. Venetia, even,
was not entirely in Italian hands; Garibaldi and a
few men (including some of the regular army) had
indeed penetrated almost to Trent, but the Italian
occupation of the Trentino was not nearly thorough
enough for Victor Emmanuel to plead " *uti
possidetis* " in favour of the Italian retention of
the district in face of Napoleon III's determined
opposition. Garibaldi was recalled.

At Vienna the Italian delegates pleaded hard for
the cession of the Trentino, with or without Italian
Tyrol, but Bismarck and Napoleon were inexorable.
Bismarck thought it might be as well for there to
remain a bone of contention between Austria and
Italy—at that time he favoured a Russian alliance
instead of an Austrian one, and thought it by no
means unlikely that when the next war came Austria
might again be Prussia's enemy—and Napoleon was
courting Francis Joseph's friendship. In October
peace was signed. By it Italy won only Venetia, and
the first clause of the treaty of peace explicitly stated
that she was indebted for that to Napoleon. One
of the conditions of the cession was that a plebiscite
of the inhabitants should be held, and the result was
overwhelmingly in favour of annexation to Italy.
Europe still retained a touching faith in plebiscites
in those days, before the events of fifty years
later showed that it was possible to influence
plebiscites by various methods, but even in the light
of this later knowledge it is impossible to doubt that,
whether influenced or not, the majority in favour of
annexation would have been enormous. At the same
time it must be admitted that a similar plebiscite in
Tyrol might very likely have rejected Italian annexa-

tion—Garibaldi had met with little support from the people during his venture, and the propaganda of the pan-Italian party had hardly begun to make headway there. The main point in favour of handing over Italian Tyrol was that the present arrangements still left Italy with a hopeless strategic frontier towards Austria; hardly as bad, perhaps, as when Austria held the Quadrilateral, but bad enough.

While Italy had to be grudgingly content with Venetia, Prussia, by virtue of Sadowa and Langensalza, was redrawing the map of Europe. Slesvig and Holstein were incorporated with Prussia, along with all Hanover and Hesse-Cassel. By these simple means not only was the subject of the original contention between Prussia and Austria wiped out, but a broad connection was at last made between Brandenburg Prussia and Rhenish Prussia, while the most likely candidate for the Empire of Germany after the King of Prussia—namely, the King of Hanover—was rendered powerless. Frankfort and Nassau went to Prussia as well, and those of her late enemies who did not suffer territorial losses were mulcted in enormous indemnities. It was hardly to be wondered at that Italy murmured.

The first matter to be settled was the trial of Persano. He had to be tried, of course, but as it happened he was a member of the Italian Upper House and claimed successfully to be tried by his peers. In English history it is well known how rarely the peers of England have convicted one of their order, and in Italy Persano had powerful friends, for the Prince of Carignano, one of the lesser Princes of the Blood, was his boon companion and largely responsible for his elevation to the supreme naval command. Persano was charged with incapacity, negligence, disobedience and cowardice, but he defended himself with skill and determination. The fate of Ramorino loomed before him; just as upon that luckless wight had been thrust the responsibility of Novara, so the Italian government was determined to make Persano responsible for all the disasters of the late war—even for Custozza, if possible.

Persano's eloquence and the influence of the Prince di Carignano saved him from the firing squad. A scanty majority in the House of Peers decided that he had not been guilty of cowardice, but found all the other charges proved—although, as Persano miserably pointed out, a man given contradictory orders must disobey one set or the other. He was cashiered, and Italian honour was to some extent satisfied.

CHAPTER XIII

ROME

IN December, 1866, the new Italian Parliament
met in Florence. There were new faces there,
for there were present the deputies from Venice.
This might be a source of pride to the nation, but
it bade fair to be also a source of woe, for it meant
that yet another potential faction was added to
the faction-torn House of Representatives. Party
struggles developed instantly. Ricasoli, the Premier,
had held his power by the grace of a number of the
more Conservative groups. Now the temper of the
electorate had veered a little round towards the Left,
and Ricasoli found himself hard put to it to maintain
his old position with his reduced majority. In despair
he appealed for help to Crispi, the Garibaldist, who
now controlled a powerful block of the moderate
Left, but Crispi declined to compromise his political
future as a Liberal by an alliance on any terms with
a Conservative. Ricasoli struggled for a space,
resigned in the hope of obtaining a larger majority
after the elections, was disappointed, and finally
handed over office to Rattazzi, the faltering Radical.

Every day the loss of Cavour was being more
deeply felt. There was no one who could control the
House as he could. When Cavour was in power the
Opposition walked warily, fearful lest he should turn
and rend them, seduce from their allegiance some
wavering block from the other side of the House,
and display himself after their attack stronger than
ever. But now nothing was so easy as opposition.

There was room enough for criticism in the government policy, and the Opposition revelled in criticism. A few vehement attacks would soon detach enough members from the government ranks to ensure the fall of the party in power, and then another block would be raised to office to enjoy for a brief space the sweets of Ministerial salaries and patronage. Their late allies, the blocks who had helped to bring this about and yet found themselves excluded from office, would then begin the whole business over again, helped by the very party which they had lately overthrown. Ministries rose and fell in bewildering succession, with the obvious result that the too frequent change of office-holders hindered the government work and made abuses more possible than they already were. Decided action was hardly to be expected of a government convinced by harsh experience that any action might well be its last.

The trouble was due to causes so many and varied that they can hardly all be discussed. One obvious point was that there was no one man now in Parliament of overwhelming personality and prestige. Cavour could always command a certain number of votes in the House, sufficient with those which the authority of the King brought over to him to force any measure through the House, but no one else could do this consistently. Crispi, Rattazzi, Ricasoli, Garibaldi, had their own small, faithful followings, but none of them could rely on the support of more than a tenth of the House. And the points at issue were so many, and the possible solutions of the problems were so varied, that it is hardly surprising that it was usually impossible to induce a majority of the House to agree to one course of action.

There were all shades of opinion concerning the best attitude towards the Church, towards the Roman State, towards France, towards Austria—all these being points vital to the very existence of the State

—as well as the natural and inevitable divergence of ideas concerning such domestic points as tariffs and the incidence of taxation. In England there is trouble enough as regards these last two points; it is difficult for the Englishman to realize the terrible sense of uncertainty which brooded over Italy at this period, with a hostile state at her heart, and two fierce and powerful enemies at her frontiers. Mazzini and the Republicans were giving continual trouble; the Church was as strong as any of the political parties, and was almost necessarily hostile; the whole structure of the State was swaying under the financial strain; and poisoning all the relations between party and party was the knowledge that partition was still a possibility, and one that would reward treason more than treason is even usually rewarded. The Englishman, with the British navy between him and the outer world, and a tradition of centuries of security behind him, can only with difficulty appreciate the maddening feeling of impermanence which sharpened the quarrels between the parties in the Italian State.

It was from her friends as much as from her enemies that Italy needed saving at this juncture. With the retirement of the Austrians from Venetia and the withdrawal of the French garrison from Rome, Victor Emmanuel was able proudly to boast in his Speech from the Throne, in 1866, that the whole peninsula was free from the foreigner. Yet therein lay the danger. Rome, abandoned by her French protectors, lay almost defenceless, open to the attacks of any filibuster who could raise a few men. The Pope was, it is true, making frantic efforts to raise a new Papal army, and Napoleon III was covertly assisting him in this most Christian project, but to men who recalled the exploits of Garibaldi and the thousand, Pius and his French and Belgian mercenaries seemed a small obstacle. Garibaldi and the extreme nationalists, overwhelmingly tempted by this tantalizing bait, clamoured for the Italian occupation

of Rome. But two years before the Italian government had signed the September convention by which
they guaranteed Pius against external aggression.
They could not go back on their pledged word, and
if they had the Emperor of the French would
assuredly have considered it a *casus belli*.   His army
was now returned from Mexico, and his military
laurels were a little smirched by the failure of the
expedition. His men would soon be in need of
occupation, and his prestige was beginning to
demand new victories.   Victor Emmanuel knew that
Napoleon would make war without hesitation, and
Custozza and Lissa had shown the risk Italy ran in
pitting herself against a first-class power.   So he
frowned upon Garibaldi's wild speeches and still
wilder plottings, and issued a proclamation calling
upon his people to refrain from headstrong actions
which would be damaging to European opinion of
Italy and would possibly lead to a fatal war with
France.

Garibaldi for once allowed his heart to overrule
his head. He was sick of international intrigues; he
was exasperated by the comparative ill success of
his campaign against Austria; he doubted Victor
Emmanuel's good faith. He believed that if he
could only lay hands on Rome then the Powers
would accept a *fait accompli*, just as they had done
when he had overrun Sicily. He was perfectly
prepared to sacrifice himself for Italy. If the Powers
disapproved, he knew he would be made a scapegoat,
but his patriotism was such that he was prepared to
make any sacrifice to break the chains that now
enslaved Rome. Garibaldi was growing more hot-
headed and impatient in his old age. He had none
of Victor Emmanuel's eternal patience, none of that
knowledge of how to wait which, the proverb says,
will bring everything in time.   Victor Emmanuel
had waited for a French quarrel with Austria before
he tried to possess himself of Lombardy; for a

Prussian quarrel with Austria before he tried to
possess himself of Venetia; he was perfectly
prepared to wait for a French quarrel with Prussia
before he tried to possess himself of Rome, especially
as he realized that he would not have long to wait.
This political insight and this profound patience was
denied Garibaldi, who impetuously decided to end
the discussion with the arguments which he knew
best how to employ—the redshirts.

In the autumn of 1867 Garibaldi began his
preparations. Money, collected from his thousands
of admirers—England sent large contributions—was
expended on rifles and artillery. The whisper went
through Italy like wildfire that Garibaldi was medita-
ting another blow for freedom, and men from all
parts of the peninsula came swarming to take part.
It was impossible for the government not to be
cognizant of what was going on. Rattazzi risked his
majority in the House, had Garibaldi arrested,
packed him off to Caprera again, and set half the
Italian navy to watch him. This act, politic though
it was, redoubled the opposition of the advanced
Liberals; the assaults of the Opposition became more
and more vehement, and the wretched Rattazzi saw
that whatever happened he would be held a fit object
for recrimination; and that he would not be able to
postpone much longer his fall from power. The
appalling news arrived that Garibaldi had made his
escape from Caprera, was established in Italy with
his redshirts round him, and was calmly proceeding
with his preparations. It was Rattazzi's duty to send
the army of Italy against him and compel him to
yield, even at the cost of another Aspromonte, but
there was no Minister in the whole of Italy who
dared to assume such a responsibility. Garibaldi was
too much a national hero for any Minister ever to
outlive the unpopularity of his defeat or his death,
and, knowing Garibaldi, Rattazzi was convinced that
he would rather die than submit tamely. There was

even the chance that he would, as a preliminary to
taking possession of Rome, possess himself of the
government of Italy. It was unlikely, but Garibaldi
would never have been so successful had he not
attempted the unlikely. Rattazzi was nearly frantic
with anxiety, and the Opposition revelled in it.
As a last desperate measure he proposed to give
Garibaldi a free hand, and to oppose by force any
possible French intervention. The proposal split his
dwindling party, and Rattazzi resigned, glad to be
free of his burden. For once there was a strange
delay in filling the vacant offices. All the leaders of
the parties in opposition showed unwonted reluctance
to assume the Nessus's cloak of the Premiership.
In the confusion of this interregnum Garibaldi
decided to strike.

By now it was October, and the situation had
altered very considerably since he had begun his
preparations in the early autumn. Pius had no
intention whatever of turning the other cheek to the
smiter, and had pushed on the organization of the
Papal army until at last he disposed of the not
inconsiderable force of thirteen thousand men.
They were well trained; some of them were honestly
fired with fanaticism over the prospect of a new
Crusade, some were intent on earning their pay, and
some were bent on satisfying their real master,
Napoleon III.

But there was a chance that Garibaldi might
encounter sterner resistance than that offered by
Pius's thirteen thousand mercenaries. Napoleon had
been watching developments in Italy with keen
intentness. The reports that had arrived of
Garibaldi's actions alarmed him, and he was in no
way reassured by the frantic notes of Rattazzi's
government. When the news came that Garibaldi
had escaped from Caprera he decided to act at once.
He would denounce the convention of September,
1864, and would send troops to sustain the Holy

Father in his principality. General de Failly was deputed to head this expedition, and arrangements for its transport were pushed on with furious energy at Marseilles.

Garibaldi had gathered his men together and had dashed for Rome. The beginning of the campaign was ominous. There had been altogether too much talk and discussion; tongues had wagged too freely, although this could hardly be Garibaldi's fault. Papal spies had wormed out some of the Garibaldist plans; notably had they discovered that the whole scheme largely hinged upon an insurrection in Rome which was to be instigated by a detachment of Garibaldists descending the Tiber with a supply of arms. Under the command of the brothers Cairoli this part of the expedition made its attempt, but the Papal police pounced upon it, brought up a regiment of French mercenaries, and destroyed the whole party at a bloody little battle of Monte Parioli. One of the Cairoli brothers fell on the field of honour, and the other died a few days later.

Garibaldi was not to be deterred by this disaster. Insurrection or no insurrection, Papal army or no Papal army, he was going through with his plans. He moved his men across the frontier, met a detachment of Papal troops at Monte Rotondo, routed them and forced them to surrender. He pushed on towards Rome, but the movement was unavailing. Pius's mercenaries held the town at their mercy, and no rising was possible within. Garibaldi was not strong enough to risk an assault, and after a week he fell back to Monte Rotondo, hoping to lure forth the Papal army and defeat them in a pitched battle.

As he wished, the Papal army moved out of Rome and came marching towards him. But Garibaldi did not know that, three days before his retreat, a French squadron had steamed into Civita Vecchia, and had landed General Failly and ten thousand French infantry and artillery. They were

close behind the Papal army, and were marching
desperately to save the Papalists from the
consequences of their rashness. As the enemy came
forward Garibaldi flung himself upon them at
Mentana. The resulting battle was fierce and
surprisingly costly. Garibaldi was beaten back, but
in turn he repulsed the Papal assaults on his line.
For a long time the battle swayed evenly, but in the
end it was decided by furious assaults on the
Garibaldist flanks made by troops which had just
arrived on the field. Before these last attacks
Garibaldi retreated, undismayed by the terrible
losses he had experienced. To him the reverse was
of no more importance than that of Monreale, when
the Neapolitans had beaten him back without prevent-
ing his obtaining possession of Palermo.

But late that night a man came riding in hot
haste into the Garibaldist camp. It was Crispi, the
man who had guided Garibaldi from that selfsame
field of Monreale, and who had headed the assault
on Palermo. Now he was head of the Liberal Party
of Italy—and a member of the Council of Action
that had sent Garibaldi into the Roman State. He
brought terrible news. The Council had discovered
what even Garibaldi had failed to ascertain even on
the field of battle.

Crispi told Garibaldi of the arrival of the French,
and his news was later confirmed by Garibaldi's
scouts. The expedition was now hopeless. Even if
Garibaldi were able to rout the Papal army and
de Failly's ten thousand men (and that was
improbable, seeing that he had just been beaten at
Mentana) it was certain that Napoleon, having once
drawn the sword, would never sheathe it as long as
a free Italian remained on Roman soil. Crispi had
acted with all the promptitude and tact expected of
the man who had held Sicily for a year against
Ferdinand II. He had wrung from Menabrea (who
had at last assumed the reins of office that Rattazzi

had let fall) a promise that no action would be taken against Garibaldi should he return into the Kingdom of Italy, and having thus made sure of a means of retreat, he had hurried to recall him.

Garibaldi yielded. The little column of redshirts, half of them wounded, all of them weary and despondent, went trailing back to the frontier, while de Failly and his triumphant infantry pressed fiercely on their rear. The pursuit ceased at the frontier, the redshirts were disbanded, and Garibaldi set out as a private person to Florence. At Figline, in defiance of his pledge, Menabrea had him arrested. He was imprisoned for a space, and then Crispi's protests bore fruit, Victor Emmanuel intervened, and he was allowed to retire to his island of Caprera.

Menabrea, of course, was between the upper and nether millstones. He had to satisfy Napoleon that Garibaldi's attempt had been made without the cognizance of the government, and he could only do that by displaying government displeasure in some marked way. Without a doubt, Napoleon would rather have seen Garibaldi shot than pardoned, but to shoot Garibaldi was more than anyone could ask of an Italian.

France was pleased by the whole business. She was delighted by de Failly's report that " the Chassepot had worked wonders " (the Chassepot was the new French breech-loading rifle in process of issue) and she was in no way averse to seeing her power demonstrated in so effective a manner. A large part of the French people genuinely desired the maintenance of the Temporal Power; of the others a number were pleasantly flattered by the knowledge that France could thus intervene in European affairs. Thus, even at the beginning of the Liberal Empire, the anachronism of Papal rule in Rome was approved in France. It was a poor substitute for the European interventions of Napoleon I—for the overlordship of the Confederation of the Rhine and the Kingdom of Italy, but it served its turn. Whether or not it was worth the enmity of Italy is a more debatable point.

With Garibaldi out of harm's way the French troops were withdrawn from Rome, but they were established permanently in Civita Vecchia, and Victor Emmanuel could no longer proudly declare that all Italy was free from the foreigner. It rankled bitterly in the minds of the Italians, and greatly strengthened the hands of the " party of action " which continued to demand the occupation of Rome.

Victor Emmanuel maintained his soul in patience and proceeded quietly with the consolidation of the dynasty and with the establishment of Italy in a definite place among the Powers. The long planned marriage between Humbert, the heir to the throne, and Margarita, daughter of that Duke of Genoa who had fought at Novara and who had died just before he could take up command of the Sardinian expeditionary force in the Crimea, took place in 1868, and with gratifying promptitude a son was born the next year. He was christened Victor Emmanuel, and at the present time he is still King of Italy.

Two years before, the King had given his consent to a marriage which had shocked many of the fervent believers in kingship, and had set an example which was only followed in a few Royal families—not till fifty years afterwards in the case of the English Royal house. He allowed his second son, Amadeus, Duke of Aosta, to marry a subject. She was of the bluest blood of Piedmont, it is true—the Princess Maria Victoria dal Pozzo della Cisterna—but she came of a Liberal family. Her princely grandfather had indeed been one of the men who had forced the constitution from Charles Albert during his unfortunate regency in 1821, and the marriage therefore had the welcome effects of healing any soreness that might still exist between the families,

M

and at the same time of gratifying the Piedmontese, who were still a little restless at the memory of the transfer of the capital from Turin to Florence. Of the marriage there were born, in quick succession, three sons, so that the House of Savoy, with its branches of Aosta, Genoa, and Carignano, was now in no danger of extinction—and that was a distinct advantage.

In international politics Victor Emmanuel found a fruitful soil to work upon. Francis Joseph of Austria, utterly defeated in 1866, had been compelled to grant some sort of constitution to his subjects, especially to the Hungarians, and in consequence he now cherished no dislike for the Kingdom of Italy on the grounds that the latter was setting a bad example to his people. The late war had shown him, too, that he could never hope to regain his old power in Germany while Italy was his enemy, and so he was very willing to give a friendly reception to Victor Emmanuel's tentative advances. Indefinite preliminaries to some sort of alliance, even, were developed, and the King's mind was relieved of all anxiety for the present regarding his north-eastern frontier.

In Germany the King met with equal success. Bismarck, working steadily towards war with France, had no desire for Italy's enmity, and fully appreciated the advantages of alliance. He cared nothing one way or the other about the future of Rome; if Victor Emmanuel wanted Rome, then he could have it as far as he was concerned. At the same time it suited Bismarck's plans that the relations between France and Italy should be as strained as possible, and he would not be ill pleased if war should develop between the two nations. Alliance with Italy to save her from the aggression of France would be a sure way of obtaining English sympathy in the coming struggle. Consequently he entered into close relations, behind Victor Emmanuel's back, with the " party of action," Crispi, Garibaldi, and the rest, for he realized that if any party was likely to force a war with France it would be this one. It is strongly to be suspected that much of the money which maintained the party of action's ceaseless activities came from Bismarck's secret service funds.

Naturally, relations between Florence and the Vatican during this period were in a state of extreme tension. Pius insisted on regarding Victor Emmanuel as a usurper, despite all the King's efforts at a reconciliation. Save on the question of the annexation of Rome, Victor Emmanuel was moderation itself. He offered to relinquish all control over the Catholic Church in Italy; he recalled the bishops who had been driven into exile some years before through their opposition to his laws for the regulation of the Church; he made offer after offer to guarantee the Pope in everything other than his sovereignty. Pius would have none of it. He eventually agreed to an interview with the King's representative for the discussion of matters connected with the Church in Italy which would not bear postponement, but he persisted in referring to the King as " King of Sardinia." He openly stated that nothing done by the House of Savoy since 1847— twenty years ago—was right or proper, and he could never be brought to recognize any of the Royal acts.

Victor Emmanuel continued with astonishing moderation. It must be borne in mind that many of Pius's acts were such as would have drawn a declaration of war from the King had they been perpetrated by any other temporal sovereign. Pius issued encyclical after encyclical condemning the Italian policy, and openly inciting Victor Emmanuel's subjects to rebellion. He encouraged the endemic brigandage of Naples and Sicily, and a dense cordon of Italian troops had to be continually maintained on the Roman frontier to restrain the bands of criminals which Pius permitted to raid Italian territory.

It almost seems as though Pius, in his old age, was suffering from delusions and megalomania. Certainly his obstinate attitude had already lost him the greater part of his influence in Austria; the Concordat of 1855 between that country and the Vatican had been abrogated during the reforms following 1866 largely through his vehement and blind opposition to those reforms. He did not realize the nature of the source of his power in France. Napoleon III was his protector solely because he believed that the support of the clerical party was necessary to the dynasty. He may have been right in this—although it is open to question— but a situation dependent on the whim of an autocrat is notoriously unstable, and doubly unstable when the position of the autocrat is insecure. The abrogation, in 1904, of the Concordat which the great Napoleon had concluded a century before, certainly seems to show that even in the 'sixties Papal influence in France was largely dependent on the Imperial policy. It seems almost incredible that Pius did not realize that the end of the Temporal Power was both near and inevitable, but it certainly seems true.

There appears to be one possible explanation. From some of the recorded utterances of Pius it seems possible that his constant study of Scripture had convinced him that the " fifty years of tribulation " were upon him. He may have honestly believed that the Book of Revelation contained references to the annexation of the Papal State. Literally interpreting this, he may have thought that Italy would yield him back Umbria, Romagna and the Marches some time in 1911, fifty years after their annexation. Whether or not he considered the dethronement of the Neapolitan Bourbons part of the tribulation of the Church it is impossible to decide.

The theory may seem absurd, but nevertheless it is of some significance that the earliest public appearances of the Pope in Rome, after the occupation, took place after 1920—fifty years from the capture of the city, when the Pope might reasonably be expected to have decided that Pius's interpretation had been exploded. Until the march of events gave back the lost provinces to Papal rule, Pius was determined to yield nothing—even if he did then.

Relations between Italy and France were in a curious state of flux. If Italy were to be in alliance with anyone at all, Victor Emmanuel personally preferred it to be France. Such an alliance would make for the security of Italy both on her land frontier and in the Mediterranean. It was obvious to everybody that a struggle between France and Prussia was close at hand, and the general consensus of military opinion was that in that event France would be victorious. Consequently it would be well to have the friendship of the greatest military Power in the world. But such friendship was impossible as long as France kept Italy out of Rome.

Consequently persistent efforts were made to induce Napoleon to abandon Pius, but to all advances Napoleon replied with a *jamais* which was as inflexible as the Papal *non possumus*. Napoleon was unduly sure of the alliance of Austria against Prussia, and he was hopeful (which with Napoleon meant usually that he thought) that the South German States would also assist him. Hanover and Hesse had only been Prussian for two or three years. He pictured to himself an irresistible French advance along the Moselle and the Lahn which would bring Bavaria over to his side and would rally to his army the Catholics of Rhineland, the Prussian Hessians and the Guelph adherents of Hanover. With such a prospect in his mind it is hardly surprising that he cared nothing for Italy's friendship or enmity. He was at no pains to conceal this galling indifference.

Generally his determined attitude towards the Roman attitude is attributed to the influence of the Empress Eugenie. Certain it is that in 1869 the Empress told the Italian premier, Menabrea, that she would never countenance the abolition of the Temporal Power. Eugenie was on her way to the opening of the Suez Canal. An eastern potentate, whose retention of power was as doubtful as was her husband's, was to entertain her with more than Oriental magnificence. Verdi, the most famous living composer, had produced a masterpiece at his invitation to celebrate the great event. Her cousin, de Lesseps, would be at the height of his fame, difficulties conquered, scandals suppressed. Eugenie could afford to be offhand towards Menabrea, however obsequiously he might bear himself. She could not read the near future when she would be dethroned, childless, and widowed, when Ismail was to be expelled with execration from Egypt, and de Lesseps was to acknowledge his failure—and worse —in Panama.

Austria treated Napoleon's suggestions of an alliance with reserve. Before committing herself she wanted to be sure of the attitudes of Russia and Italy. Russia was non-committal; Bismarck had made sure of her neutrality (friendship with Russia was the keystone of his foreign policy) and Austria could not be quite sure that in the event of war between Prussia and herself she would not enter into the conflict as Prussia's active ally. Yet she was almost prepared to risk that, in view of the tempting bait dangled before her of the overlordship of Germany, as long as Italy could be kept quiet. She was far less fitted for a war on two fronts than was Prussia. Accordingly she approached Italy—and once more there developed the question of Rome.

Austria implored Napoleon to hand over the city, and Napoleon was still recalcitrant. It is possible that at that moment, had Napoleon reversed his Roman policy, he would have gained the alliance both of Austria and Italy.

Later, affairs changed for the worse, from Napoleon's point of view. Keen critics were counting battalions and weighing mobilization arrangements. The Austrian and Italian military attachés suddenly began to incline to the opinion that the Imperial army was only a Colossus stuffed with clouts. Heretical though it was, at that period, to doubt French military efficiency, there was a growing body of expert opinion that matters were not as well as they might be in the French army. There was no doubting the terrific power of the Prussians. Moltke had proved himself, in 1866, the foremost general of the age. The only French Marshal to compare with him, Niel, was dying. The others, Macmahon, Bazaine, Leboeuf, were all men only of second rate talent. That the Emperor should command in person would be what the enemies of France would most desire. The whisper grew in cabinets and war offices that perhaps Prussia would be successful in the approaching struggle. At once Austria's friendship began to cool. Italy began to see her way clear. If France beat Prussia she would not be allowed to take possession of Rome; if Prussia beat France there would be none to stop her. Certainly, then, she would not help France; rather should she consider the advisability of allying herself with Prussia against her. But this last was a step too far. Belief in the military power of France was too deeply rooted in unenlightened circles for such a step to be popular; the whole weight of clerical influence was in favour of Napoleon, and there was still some slight trend of public opinion, dating from the victories of 1859, in the same direction.

The negotiations dragged on. Austria was not

ready for war (the reforms following 1866 were not yet completed) and proposed that Italy should be France's active ally while she merely made ready to support the allies when they appeared across the Rhine. Italy counterproposed that it should be Austria that did the fighting while she determined her attitude according to that of Russia. Under these circumstances the negotiations were reduced to a farce, and nothing could be satisfactorily settled.

Meanwhile Bismarck was moving steadily forward towards his objective. He guessed—or his secret service discovered—the proposals and counterproposals of Austria and Italy, and he realized that as long as Prussia was victorious he had nothing to fear from them. He was sure (despite Napoleon's theories) of the assistance of all Germany. And he was positive that Prussia would be victorious in the coming struggle. It only remained to arrange matters so that it would appear that it was France who was the aggressor.

In matters of diplomacy Napoleon and his assistants, de Grammont, Ollivier, and the others, were as powerless as children in Bismarck's hands. Niel and de Morny, who might have helped the Emperor, were both dead. In an ill-advised moment the Ollivier government decided to try once more their old method of bolstering up French prestige. It was one which had been highly successful, with Italy as the victim, on several occasions. A Prince of the House of Hohenzollern had been elected to the throne of Spain. France took alarm—fairly unreasonable alarm — at the suggestion, and demanded the withdrawal of the candidature. William of Prussia obligingly saw that the withdrawal was carried into effect, although he declined to admit that he could offer more than advice to the young man in question or to his father. The French Foreign Office would have none of this. France was in need of a diplomatic victory. A well-worded snub to her most powerful neighbour would be gratifying to a nation which expected such things from her Emperor (in rather the same way as another nation had once demanded circuses) and strict instructions were sent to Benedetti, the French Ambassador, to demand from William of Prussia a promise that the candidature would not be renewed. William, disturbed in his holiday at Ems by the pertinacious Benedetti, briefly replied that the candidature had been withdrawn, and, as far as he could see, was unlikely to be renewed. Nevertheless, because (as he had already pointed out) he was not responsible for the actions of the Prince in question, he could not make any further promise, and he saw no purpose in continuing the discussion.

Bismarck, von Moltke and von Roon, dining together in Berlin, received the telegram which faithfully recounted this interview between King and Ambassador. Between them they deftly edited it, so that it appeared that the King's final remarks had been a not too mannerly dismissal. Bismarck inserted the revised telegram (which still told the truth, however much it suggested what had never happened) in the *Berlin Express*, and waited events. Two days later the Paris papers were shrieking that the French Ambassador had been insulted, and clamoured, one and all, for redress and apology. Mild little Benedetti, quietly holiday-making, was astonished to learn that he had been treated with contumely at Ems, and was spurred by a series of bellicose telegrams from Paris to demand reparation. He did his duty as well as he was able, and Berlin met him with a delighted inflexibility. No apology could Benedetti exact; the next telegram abruptly ordered him to ask for his passports. A French officer was on the way to Berlin bearing a declaration of war. The Chassepot and the *zundnadel* were to fight the matter out.

In Florence the news was received with mixed

feelings.   The Francophiles demanded an immediate
alliance with France; the blind believers in the
French army thought timidly that such an arrangement would be the best insurance against the future;
Sella and Visconti-Venosta, the keenest minds in
the Italian cabinet, vehemently opposed any such
suggestion.   Once more Austria and Italy sounded
Napoleon as to Rome.   Once more there came the
eternal answer—" *Jamais.*"   The question of alliance
was again shelved for the moment.

Later, Napoleon's attitude gradually changed.
Early in August he discovered that the *archiprêt*
army of which Leboeuf had boasted was the very
reverse of ready.   The German mobilization was
proceeding steadily and inexorably.   In a spasm of
doubt he recalled his troops from Civita Vecchia,
and informed the Italian Ambassador at Paris that
he would not be unwilling to see an Italian *corps
d'armée* side by side with his own men, as in the
great days of Magenta and Solferino.   But he made
no promise about Rome, and the hint was ignored.
The " stage thunder " of the Prince Imperial's
baptism of fire at Sarrebruck deceived no one.   It was
growing evident that the French army was faced
with a terrible defeat.   Then there came, posthaste,
an Ambassador Extraordinary to Florence.   It
was the Prince Napoleon, the husband of Victor
Emmanuel's own daughter Clothilde.   Clearly it
must be a matter of import which sent such a man
on an errand.   Napoleon bore with him a sheet of
paper, blank save for the Imperial signature.   He
offered it to Victor Emmanuel in the presence of
his cabinet, saying, " Fill in what you please."
Napoleon III was now ready to grant anything if
only Italy would give him help.

But Italy was as well aware of the reason for this
change of front as was Napoleon himself.   News
had come flashing over the wire.   It was the news
that the Empire was tottering.   It was the news of

Macmahon's defeat at Woerth.　Austria and Italy combined in their reply to the Ambassador Extraordinary : " Too late."

The Prussian armies came swooping over the Rhine.　Macmahon was beaten at Woerth ; Frossard was beaten at Spicheren ; Bazaine clung to Metz until it was too late.　He beat vainly at the bars ; at Colombey, at Vionville, at Gravelotte his desperate attempts to escape were foiled by the vigour and self-devotion of the German battalions.　Macmahon, spurred forward by frantic orders from Paris to do something to save the dynasty, collected a motley host around the nucleus which had escaped from Woerth, and went plunging forward to utter ruin ; with him was Napoleon.

In Italy, meanwhile, events were moving with tremendous rapidity.　For the past year Rome had been full of the higher dignitaries of the Church, summoned by Pius to an Ecumenical Council.　They had made several pronouncements, none of them of overwhelming importance, but at last they had come to a decision on a point of faith which had for a long time since occupied the attention of the Catholic world.　On the day of the declaration of the Franco-Prussian War this decision was announced.　It stated, briefly, that any announcement that the Pope made *ex cathedra* must be true and correct.　There is no need to debate the matter—it has been done *ad nauseam* both by scoffers and by the sincere—but it might be as well to point out that this adoption of the new dogma is some sort of confirmation of the theory that Pius was suffering from acute megalomania.

The Church itself was divided.　Not so much upon the question of the intrinsic trustworthiness of this dogma of Papal infallibility—although many people had heterodox opinions on the point, notably in Germany, where a considerable sect broke away from the Church—but on that of the advisability of promulgating the decision at such a time. Manning, the English Cardinal, and one of the keenest (some said one of the most worldly) minds in all the College, was emphatic in his condemnation. But Pius insisted, and the dogma of the Papal infallibility became part of the Catholic Faith. It was not realized then, as it is now, that no one really knows when the Pope is speaking *ex cathedra*—he is not bound to declare whether he is or not—and so the situation remains unchanged. The announcement had no effect on Victor Emmanuel; his army waited patiently on the frontier for an opportunity to thrust this infallible Pope from his temporal throne.

The news of Woerth and Gravelotte, and of the withdrawal of the garrison from Civita Vecchia, brought consternation to Rome, and the Ecumenical Council broke up in confusion. Cardinals and Bishops made the best of their way homewards, anxious to be out of the Eternal City at the time, so obviously near at hand now, when the Bersaglieri would come marching to the Quirinal. Pius waited in a state of profound mental agitation.

Suddenly there appeared a new character on the stage. Mazzini had realized that the French government was powerless to interfere with his plans in Italy, and he had called upon his followers to erect once more the Republic of Rome. All through Italy attempts were to be made to raise the standard of revolt, but the main effort was planned for Rome. It did not succeed. Victor Emmanuel's secret service had the matter well in hand. Mazzini, rashly landing in Sicily, was seized, put on board a man-of-war, and promptly shut up in the fortress of Gaeta. Pius's fifteen thousand mercenaries were able to hold down the attempts in Rome, and the other demonstrations in Lombardy and the Marches were speedily checked. The capture of Mazzini ended, as soon as it was begun, a rising in Calabria which might well, under other circumstances, have set all

that most distressful province in a blaze. Yet the
agitation was sufficient to show that Italy was in a
state of subdued turmoil; it was the King's duty to
make a move, and at once.

The first week of September brought important
news. Macmahon at Chalons, blinded by his
devotion to the Imperial house, had obeyed the
orders of Count Palikao against his better judgment;
he had tried to release Bazaine from Metz; forced
northwards and westwards by overwhelming numbers
he had been hemmed in at Sedan against the Belgian
frontier. Napoleon was with him. The latter, in
a last endeavour to free Macmahon's hands (and
perhaps with other motives as well), had sent in his
personal surrender to William of Prussia. Next day
Macmahon was wounded, and his successor, after a
few hours of command-in-chief, yielded to the
inevitable and surrendered the whole force. The last
field army of France, over eighty thousand strong,
was marched away to the interior of Germany.

In Paris the defeat bore its expected fruit. The
dynasty fell, and the Republic was proclaimed from
the Hôtel de Ville. However the war progressed, or
even if it were now to end, there was no possibility
whatever of armed interference in Italy on the part
of France. Victor Emmanuel sent forward his
waiting regiments.

Even now Pius had no intention of submitting
tamely. His mercenaries were given strict orders to
oppose the invasion. But forty thousand Royalists
entered the Roman State, and the Papal army could
do little. Bixio, once one of Garibaldi's henchmen,
swept round by Viterbo in a bold endeavour to catch
the Papal army outside Rome and drive it away
from the city, but the difficult enterprise met with
undeserved failure. Civita Vecchia, with its garrison
of fifteen hundred, surrendered to him, and then
the whole Royal army concentrated round Rome.
Cadorna, the commander-in-chief, demanded the

submission of the city; Kanzler, Pius's lieutenant, replied with dignity, denying that the people of Rome desired a change of masters, and affirming that he and his men would die at their posts in the defence of the city.

The last thing which Victor Emmanuel desired was a storming and a possible sack of the city; he did not wish to celebrate the occupation of his new capital with a shedding of blood. Cadorna, by his orders, set gingerly about his task. It was the King's design not to occupy the Leonine city, but to leave that to Pius as a last relic of his temporal power. Consequently it was on this side that a feigned attack was made, pushed just far enough to draw some of the defence away from the scene of the real assault. Then the guns blew in the wall at the Porta Pia, and the troops rushed forward to the attack. There was a brief skirmish, and then, at last, the white flag was hung out. Pius retired to the Vatican, and the Italian army occupied all Rome save for the Leonine city.

There is a fantastic story to the effect that Pius really meant to hold the city to the last, and that the officer responsible for the surrender, in after years, rashly visiting the Vatican, was seized at the Pope's orders and actually executed for his breach of trust. If this ever happened, Pius would be perfectly justified under any military code, especially as he still regarded himself as an independent monarch in the Vatican, but there does not seem to be a word of truth in the whole legend.

CHAPTER XIV

VICTOR EMMANUEL'S LAST YEARS

VICTOR EMMANUEL showed no haste to enter in person his new province. The military government of Rome was left to Cadorna, who arranged for the evacuation of the Leonine city by the Papal army, and the march of the latter to Civita Vecchia and its shipment out of Italy.

No sooner had they gone when an incident occurred which threw a curious light upon Kanzler's declaration that Rome did not want Victor Emmanuel. The news had leaked out that the King intended leaving to Pius all the Leonine city, cutting it off from the rest of Rome and from the Kingdom of Italy. At once the population rose, threatening revolt unless they, too, were admitted to union with Italy. The situation grew so menacing that Pius had to swallow his pride, and, for his own personal protection, send a nuncio to Cadorna asking him to occupy the Leonine city as well. The Vatican and Lateran were all that now remained to Pius.

Examination of contemporary accounts of Rome during this period of transition is vastly disturbing to the historian's belief in the innate truthfulness of humanity. The general rule is systematic, flagrant contradiction. Eminent churchmen solemnly declare that all Rome was plunged in mourning; that the whole population heartily regretted Cadorna's arrival; that the fall of the Temporal Power was the death-blow to Roman happiness. Some observations from

the laity confirm this. On the other hand, official
statements (the authority is put forward with due
reserve), abundant private and public accounts, and
not a few statements of clergy, say that it was a
period of wild carnival; that Rome had never been
so delighted as when the political exiles, who had
fled before pontifical persecution, re-entered the
city; and that the general atmosphere of relief was
unmistakable. It is barely possible that both sides
are right. The Papalists, hardly moving out from
the Vatican and its environs, were continually
plunged in gloom, and may not have observed the
festivities (it seems beyond all doubt that there *were*
festivities) of the rest of the city. However it was,
the results of the plebiscite, which soon began to
come in, seemed to prove for certain that the
population of the Roman State desired union with
Italy. Nevertheless, as has been pointed out before,
plebiscites never constitute absolute proof; it must
be remembered that there was an Italian army
in occupation, which would have been hugely
embarrassed had any other result been reached.

Of one thing there is no doubt at all, and that
is that under Papal rule the Romans had sunk to the
lowest depths of political and even mental inanition.
Crude misgovernment, a system of justice whereby
the good Catholic escaped the penalty of his
misdeeds, while the suspected heretic or Liberal
paid twofold, and a reactionary policy which drove
all the best intellects in flight to other parts of the
peninsula, had reduced the mass of the people to a
poverty-stricken, unthinking horde, without initiative
or hope. Vice was rampant, illiteracy was the rule,
and intelligence the exception.

The plebiscite declared unreservedly for annexation to the Kingdom of Italy. Pius and his
supporters protested against the indignity to which
the Head of the Church was exposed in being thus
turned out of his own kingdom by his own people,

but the protests went unheeded. They were a last desperate attempt to enlist the sympathy of the Powers. France was in no condition to consider other people's troubles; Austria was anxious to gain Italy's goodwill; Russia had no interest at all in the Pope, and was perhaps by no means displeased with the rise of a new Power in the Mediterranean, which might counterbalance the influence of Austria or Turkey; while England displayed both sympathy with Italy and antipathy to the Pope.

During the winter of 1870-71 the Parliament at Florence was mainly occupied with the task of assimilating the new territory to the kingdom, and with trying to define the position of the Pope. The new legislation was based upon suggestions found in Cavour's papers after his death—Cavour had died with the words " A free Church in a free State " on his lips. The terms offered were heroically generous. The Pope was guaranteed in his possession of the Vatican, the Lateran, and minor properties, which were to be considered extra-territorial in the same manner as are embassies. In consideration of his " cession " of the Roman State he was to receive the not inconsiderable income of over a hundred thousand pounds sterling a year, and separate postal and telegraphic facilities were put at his disposal. He was to be treated as a crowned head, and was to receive in public the same honours as were accorded the King himself. He was invited to maintain a body of personal guards. It was even promised that letters and telegrams to the Pope should be transmitted without charge.

To the Church, as distinct from the Pontiff, Victor Emmanuel made offers equally generous. He waived his right to nominate the higher functionaries of the Church (no other monarch in Europe had done that), and he agreed that these should not be asked to take the oath of allegiance to him. He agreed that all proclamations and decisions of the Church

N

should be made public without being subject to his veto or revision. Lastly, he acknowledged that the State had no right to interfere in matters of spiritual discipline.

Privately Victor Emmanuel hinted that he would have no objection to Pius continuing to lay formal claim to the sovereignty of Rome, provided matters went no further. For a good many years Pius had been content with no more in the case of Avignon —Napoleon III had ruled Avignon and yet Pius had raised no public objection.

Yet to all these offers the Papal court returned the well-worn answer, "*Non possumus.*" Pius shut himself up in the Vatican, declared he was a prisoner, and never luxuriated in the proffered "royal honours" for the simple reason that he never appeared in public. He even kept up the stale farce of never alluding to Victor Emmanuel save as King of Sardinia, and he never touched a penny of his hundred thousand a year.

Victor Emmanuel wanted to see Cardinals in the Upper House of his Parliament; Pius blandly declared there was no such parliament and, in addition, rather inconsistently, refused to allow the Cardinals to sit there. He carried out the principle to its logical extreme (a logical extreme is usually a logical absurdity), with the result that no one of the Papal faction could ever recognize the existence of a Royalist, and Roman society became sharply divided into the two sections of Papalists and Royalists, never coming into contact, never acknowledging the other, and with never a chance of healing the wound. To this day there are "Blacks" and "Whites" in Rome, and the division is only just beginning to close.

Crispi and the Left opposed the arrangement tooth and nail. It was only natural that they should do so, perhaps, seeing that they were in opposition, but they found many specious arguments in their support. They denounced the whole arrangement as too generous, and they declared that for Italy to allow in her midst the existence of an undoubtedly hostile power with great political influence was sheer madness. Extremists wanted to see all trace of the Papacy erased from the peninsula. Victor Emmanuel had too much common sense to listen to their arguments. He realized that Pius, with his fanatical obstinacy, would not consent to " go quietly." To turn the Pope out of Italy would call for physical force—impious hands would have to be laid upon His Holiness before he could be removed from the country. And that would never do. It would excite a revulsion of feeling in favour of the Pope just at the critical time. Since Pius had to stay in Italy, it would be as well to make a virtue of necessity and be as generous as possible, so as to give him small grounds for complaint.

There is no doubt that the King acted wisely. Approval of his measures was general throughout Europe; it was only by a hair's breadth that he failed to secure formal recognition of the " law of guarantees " by the governments of his neighbours. The King's justification lies in the fact that the re-establishment of the Temporal Power has never been suggested seriously, and that neither the personal popularity of the Pope nor his influence have ever overshadowed those of the King of Italy.

The " law of guarantees " was one of the last labours of the Florence Parliament. In June, 1871, Victor Emmanuel made his formal entry into Rome, amid scenes of wild enthusiasm. Only twelve years ago he had been merely King of Sardinia, of less weight in the world than his colleague of Naples, and certainly less important than the Kings of Bavaria or of Hanover. Now Francis was a discredited refugee; the King of Hanover had fallen to the rank of an English duke; the King of Bavaria was subject to the German Emperor, while Victor

Emmanuel, with his twenty-five millions of subjects, took his place on equality with any ruler in the world. Much had happened since Novara.

Into Rome there now poured a host of people of all classes—the followers of the Court and of the Parliament; needy adventurers; speculators both needy and wealthy. Without trade or industries, Rome nevertheless began to expand rapidly. The expansion was due solely to the facts that the town was so much visited by tourists, was the seat of government, and was the residence of two Courts, yet it has been maintained to this day. In many ways this is perhaps unfortunate. With the increase in size of the town, and the swelling of the volume of the traffic, new roads are having to be continually cut, with the result that the appearance of the town is changing—and not for the better, say many. The old monuments are vanishing, or are being set up incongruously in streets of modern appearance; some, inevitably, are being destroyed. There are many who sigh for the opportunity to see the Capitol as it was before the erection of the monument to Victor Emmanuel; the Bank of Italy is unworthy of the Via Nazionale; the planning of the Corso Vittorio Emmanuele and the embankment of the river necessarily swept away an enormous amount of vastly interesting material. It is the price Italy has to pay for union—and for the Romans the pill is gilded by the fourfold increase in the price of land in Rome since the annexation.

Hardly had the government settled down in the new capital when the Tiber rose in flood; the mortality and destruction were enormous. It was the worst flood in history, and the Papal party gloomily attributed it to the impiety of the people in allowing the disinheritance of the Vicar of Christ. The government, however, considered that it was far more probably due to centuries of gross mismanagement by Papal public works departments. It proceeded to make a similar disaster unlikely in the future, serenely ignoring the mutterings of the Church. Indeed, the resolute fashion in which Victor Emmanuel in the Quirinal and Pius in the Vatican each refused to recognize the other's existence was amusing in its consistency. They lived less than two miles apart for a period of eight years—like Gilbert's two castaways :

> " When they meet each other now
> They cut each other dead."

Yet now the occupation at last made possible a wholehearted attempt to consolidate Italy into a single nation. Francis of Bourbon (called by the faithful King of the Two Sicilies) had hurriedly left Rome when Cadorna entered it. He was now a wanderer in Austria, and an end had come to his plottings and meddlings in the southern provinces. The extensive criminal class which had flourished under the kindly rule of Pius was now subject to the rule of a police force which could boast zeal and organization. The brigandage of Calabria and the Abruzzi was cut off at the source. It seemed as though the Golden Age was about to be inaugurated.

But even now the difficulties were enormous. With the attainment of the national ambition, troubles between parties in the State and the rivalries between the provinces became more acute than ever. The growing manufacturing interests of the north clamoured for State assistance, by tariffs or otherwise; the agricultural interests of the south wanted none of these things. The Liberals demanded an extension of the franchise and democratic innovations of all kinds; the Conservatives gloomily wondered whether they had not gone too far already. Mazzini maintained his activities (all tending towards disruption), and the mantle of

Garibaldi, now that he had returned from his abortive expedition to the help of the French Republic a confirmed invalid, had fallen upon the shoulders of men hardly awake to all their responsibilities. And those of us who have seen all the customers in an Italian café rise to their feet and remain standing while one of the survivors of the Thousand entered and found himself a seat, will realize the almost unbounded influence of the Garibaldi tradition in Italy.

Budgeting difficulties were large. There was an extensive paper currency of forced circulation, while no ministry could be found with the hardihood to impose taxation which would enable the national income to balance its expenditure. For a time the Conservative Party in power made both ends meet by the simple process of selling off confiscated ecclesiastical property—a policy open to the twofold objection that it was impermanent while affording unbounded openings to the criticism of the Opposition. It became more and more evident that the continuance in power of the Right was precarious, and this affected the national credit disadvantageously, thanks to Mazzini's manœuvres, which made the lending public suspicious of the designs of the Left.

And now came France once more to fish in the troubled Italian waters in the hope of recapturing her old paramount position in the peninsula. 1870 had left her weak, and she could not hope to profit by force of arms, but there was an extensive field open for the employment of diplomatic measures. France had two valuable allies in Italy—the goodwill of the Church and the traditional sympathy of the Italians, recently strengthened by Garibaldi's expedition. Yet she could achieve nothing. The Church was still discredited, and to counterbalance the French military ascendancy Victor Emmanuel found far more potent allies.

FRANCESCO CRISPI

Austria now had no reason to dislike Italy. With the victories of Custozza and Lissa to her credit, she could afford to bear no malice for Italy's part in the late war, and as she had now granted constitutional reforms she could not look upon Italy as setting a bad example in this matter. The approaching clash of Austrian and Russian interests in the Balkans made it imperative that Austria should be sure of Italy's friendship. The natural consequence was that Francis Joseph tendered a polite invitation to Victor Emmanuel to visit him at his capital during the Vienna Exhibition, and the invitation was accepted.

King and ministers accordingly spent a week in Vienna, and here was conceived the beginning of the Triple Alliance, which was to establish Italy as one of the Powers of Europe and to counterbalance French influence in the peninsula. Friendship with Austria had already begun to mean friendship with the German Empire. Although Bismarck was still in power, and still worked desperately hard to retain the alliance of Russia in preference to that of Austria, there was not wanting an influential party who inclined to the belief that by alliance with Russia Germany lost more than she gained. And whether Russia were a friend or an enemy, Germany, with France displaying marvellous powers of recuperation after the recent defeat, could not afford to be on other than good terms with Italy. Consequently the old Emperor received Victor Emmanuel with all the courtesy and kindliness at his command, while the King's bluff honesty in admitting the fact that he had been near to being France's ally in 1870, and in stating the reasons for his eventual neutrality, went far towards clearing up any possible misunderstanding. From the visit of Victor Emmanuel to Berlin in 1873 may be dated that alteration in the attitude of Germany towards Russia, which later had so profound an influence upon the history of civilization.

Two years later the matter progressed a step further, when the two Emperors came at short intervals to pay visits to the King. They could not come to Rome—there would have been awkward complications about the Vatican, for Francis Joseph, at least, could hardly visit Rome and yet not pay his respects to the Head of his Church—and consequently did not cross the Appenines. Francis Joseph actually selected as his place of sojourn Venice, which for decades past had cursed his name. Shades of Daniel Manin! His Imperial, Royal, and Apostolic Majesty sailed in a State gondola up the Grand Canal, and landed amid cheers in the shadow of St. Mark, from whence so many proclamations vowing eternal hatred of him and his house had been issued. The Republicans condemned the visit as a solemn farce in the worst of taste, but most of Italy was flattered and delighted.

Farce or not, with Austria a firm ally and French influence neutralized, Italy was now in a far stronger position. There were plenty of straws to show which way the wind blew. Garibaldi at last became reconciled to the King, and no longer allowed memories of Aspromonte to embitter their relations. He consented to take the oath of allegiance to the Crown, and to assume his seat in the Chamber of Deputies—he had steadily absented himself since the cession of Savoy. Many Republicans followed his example. Some time before—in March, 1872—a mysterious Mr. Brown had died at Pisa. He was apparently an Englishman with his residence at Lugano, but the Italian police knew more about him than that. He was really an Italian, who had often been at loggerheads with the government, and who had not only declined the amnesty offered him but had also consistently refused to avail himself of the seat in Parliament which was rightfully his. His name was Giuseppe Mazzini.

The Republicans gave him as splendid a funeral

as they could manage, but they realized even then that with Mazzini's death the strength of his party had departed. Mazzini's admirers can point to very little enduring proof of the importance of his work— he is remembered almost more now as a critic than as an agitator—but that is characteristic of his career. An idealist, and a selfless one, he was born to point the way rather than to create. To him is the merit of having been one of the earliest men who combined the conviction that Italy should be united, with the courage to declare it. His eloquence rallied the lukewarm to the cause, and his eternal patience was proof against all the setbacks of 1830 and 1848. His most valuable work was done in the earlier part of the century, when words were of as much value as swords —it can hardly be imputed to him as a fault that his ideas ran contrary to those of Victor Emmanuel. Mazzini was by temperament a Republican; Victor Emmanuel was by birth a King. Mazzini was reckless and impractical, but he was energetic, patient, incorruptible, and supremely eloquent. It was thanks to Victor Emmanuel that Italy made the best use of him.

The temporary ruin of the Republican party, caused by the death of Mazzini and the reconciliation of Garibaldi to the King, was followed by a sigh of relief through Italy. The bogey of anarchy and civil war removed, there was no longer so deadly a fear of the Liberal party. The Conservatives were unable to stave off the inevitable. The Liberal elements in the House combined spasmodically, and eventually Minghetti resigned in face of repeated Parliamentary defeats. The ensuing elections brought Crispi at last into power, with a programme which promised (in the way programmes have) the new millennium. Crispi had broken definitely with the Republicans, and consequently was assured of the Royal support. "The Monarchy unites us when the Republic would divide us," said Crispi, and there is no doubt that at that time he was correct. Italy was not yet welded together sufficiently to be able to dispense with a monarchical form of government; if the Republicans had had their way it seems most likely that in a few years Italy would have travelled down the same steep and slippery path as the South American Republics.

Crispi, as the man who had once ruled Sicily, as the supporter of Garibaldi, with a reputation for honesty which was thoroughly well deserved, brought to his party a prestige equalled by that of no other living Italian politician. He had an overpowering majority, and his supporters were flushed with their recent success. He was certainly free to inaugurate the new millennium if he and his followers were equal to the task. He was not—and his supporters were still less so. Circumstances compelled Crispi to act on the assumption that men who had been brigadiers under Garibaldi, or who had suffered imprisonment under Ferdinand II or Pius IX would be sound constructive statesmen; too soon he discovered the error, and proved that a lifetime spent in opposition is no qualification for high office.

The earliest justification, in the eyes of the public, of the Liberal party, was the abolition of the grist-tax, which was the staple source of Italian revenue and at the same time the most objectionable impost in the opinion of the public. The matter was badly managed, and the grain-dealers were well organized. The abolition in the tax brought no reduction in the price of flour—but it brought unending confusion to the Treasury and a welcome additional profit to the grain-dealers. The failure was ominous.

But Crispi, Nicotera, and Cairoli struggled valiantly on. The redemption of the forced paper currency had to be postponed in consequence of the grist-tax fiasco, and false economies which were resorted to in naval and military affairs left their mark nearly permanently on the services, but nevertheless a good deal of headway was made. Victor Emmanuel, anxiously watching the result of their efforts, began to realize that his forecast was correct, and that a Liberal ministry was at least of no more danger to the State than was a Conservative one.

The King's task was now nearly finished. He had united Italy, and he had employed his influence to such effect that he had been able to give his country the form of government that would be most likely to endure. In office now was the most capable politician and man of action available; one, too, whose position was such that he could call justifiably for support from all the parties in the State. It almost seemed as though the King's burning patriotism led him to choose this moment for his death, as the best for Italy that would be likely to occur for some time.

One by one the men who made Italy were dropping away. Mazzini was dead; Cavour was dead; early in January, 1878, came the turn of La Marmora. He had seen much, done much. He had commanded a division under Charles Albert at Custozza, and under Chrzanowsky at Novara. To him had been entrusted the difficult tasks of the pacification of Genoa in 1849 and of Calabria from 1861-66. He had won for Italy her first real victory —that of the Tchernaya. He had carried through the alliance with Prussia in 1866. Now he had to yield to old age.

The news of his death was brought to Victor Emmanuel at Rome. It was a grave shock to him; La Marmora was almost the last of his old comrades in arms. At the moment Crispi and the King were engaged on a delicate task. They were making arrangements for the Pope's funeral. True, Pius was not yet dead, but trustworthy information had trickled through from the Vatican that he was seriously ill, and it was well to be prepared. Hardly

had Victor Emmanuel approved of Crispi's suggestions than he took to his bed, struck down by the
fever endemic in Rome.　Victor Emmanuel had
never cared for Rome, and an old prophecy had
declared that the city would be his death.

The prophecy proved correct.　The news of
Victor Emmanuel's illness had hardly been conveyed
to a horror-struck people than it was followed by the
news of his death.　He died a month before the
Pope, whose funeral procession he had just arranged.

Grim stories were told of his end.　Pius, on his
deathbed, heard of his mortal illness, and, with a last
flicker of the Christian spirit he tried to send one of
his Cardinals to him with a message of forgiveness.
The Cardinal was too much of a diplomat to give such
a message in public—it would be damaging to the
Papal cause.　The Court would on no account allow
him a private interview with the dying King.　They
feared lest he might wring from him some admission
of regret for occupation of Rome, and that would
never do.　The King died unreconciled to the Head
of his Church, and Pius, in his last hours, bewailed
the fact that he was unable to leave his bed; had it
been otherwise, he declared feebly to his perturbed
Cardinals, he would have abandoned his policy of
seclusion on which the Church relied so much, and
come in person on his errand of forgiveness.　The
Court could hardly have denied *him* admission.

The King was hardly dead; young Humbert had
hardly succeeded to the throne (quietly, thanks to
Crispi's influence exerted from the Home Office)
when a deputation arrived posthaste from Turin.　It
demanded that the King should be buried along with
his fathers, in the Superga, in the grave he had
himself planned earlier in his life, before Rome fell
into his hands.　Crispi refused.　The Romans and
the Neapolitans rallied to his side.　All the dormant
jealousy between north and south flamed out on the
instant.　Over Victor Emmanuel's dead body was

INAUGURATION OF THE MONUMENT IN ROME TO VICTOR EMMANUEL II

JUNE 4TH, 1912

fought a fight as bitter as that waged for the body of Patroclus.

Crispi averred that the seizure of Rome was Victor Emmanuel's crowning exploit, and that it was right that his bones should remain there, in the capital won by his vigour and determination. The Piedmontese counterclaimed that they should lie beside those of Charles Albert, along with those of his brothers, in the temple which had for eight hundred years sheltered the mortal remains of the Princes of the House of Savoy.

Even in Parliament was the sordid question fought out. The site of the grave of the greatest King Italy had ever seen was determined by a decision of the Chamber of Deputies—the groups coalesced and split up over the matter in the usual style. Piedmont was outnumbered and outvoted. From Tuscany southwards Italy was determined that Victor Emmanuel should not rest with his fathers. There could be no two opinions as to where, if not in Turin, his grave should be. When the discussion was finished Victor Emmanuel found a resting-place in the Pantheon, Hadrian's eighteen hundred year old temple, dedicated by a seventh century Pope to Saint Mary of the Martyrs.

There his grave is still to be seen; his memory is still green; but the tradition that he left has been cut short.

CHAPTER XV

THE KING

THERE is no one in history to whom Victor Emmanuel can be aptly compared; not to Cæsar, nor to Augustus, nor to Charlemagne, nor to Louis XI, nor to James I, nor to Wilhelm I, and most certainly not to either of the two Napoleons. Perhaps the reason is that he was more honest than these.

Cognomens, affixed officially or by acclamation, in the main are as untruthful as are epitaphs. The " Greats " and the " Well-beloveds " and the " Martyrs " of history often appear to the unprejudiced eye very much the reverse. But there has never arisen a whisper to the effect that the Re Galantuomo was not all that his people believed him to be.

He has his detractors, of course. He was not popular in French diplomatic circles—that was hardly to be expected, seeing that French diplomacy over Italian questions failed as lamentably as it did in Germany—and, both during his lifetime and after his death, spiteful little books appeared in France full of succulent details about the " barbarism " of the man who outwitted the Second Empire.

It is the " barbarism " about which the books have most to say. They sneer subtly at the King because he thought more about his army than about art or about the pleasures of the table—forgetting that had their Emperor looked after his army better

the German regiments would not bear the names of
Gravelotte and Sedan on their standards. As for art
—it hardly seems a matter for sneering that a man
should not be interested in the art that prevailed
between 1849 and 1878. It hardly seems disparaging
to Victor Emmanuel to say that he did not
patronize Winterhalter.

There seems to be no disadvantage in a King's
preference of onions to truffles, or of the society of
huntsmen to that of courtiers. Actually, the King's
homely tastes were assets of the nation. Upon
the personal affection of the Italians for Victor
Emmanuel hung the fate of Italy. In Naples or in
Tuscany his thousand year old ancestry availed him
not at all. A Savoyard might die for him because
fifty of his grandfathers had ruled Savoy; a
Florentine would find it a more cogent reason that
he enjoyed polenta, and a Calabrian bandit that he
was happiest on the mountains.

Victor Emmanuel was unhappy in his childhood.
He was as unlike his father, Charles Albert, as it was
possible to be. In place of Charles Albert's blonde,
aquiline good looks and tall slim figure, Victor
Emmanuel could only boast a snub nose, a black
moustache, and a height hardly above the average.
Charles Albert was a sincere Catholic verging upon
bigotry; Victor Emmanuel was a sincere Catholic
verging upon scepticism. Charles Albert preferred
words to action; Victor Emmanuel preferred action
to words. The father was an autocrat by instinct
and a democrat by persuasion; the son's opinions can
best be described as political atheism (the term is
inevitable) tempered by common sense.

Obviously there were many possible sources of
trouble between father and son, and the situation
was made more tense by the fact that Victor
Emmanuel's younger brothers were more like his
father. Ferdinand, Duke of Genoa, and Otho, who
died quite young, were Charles Albert's favourites.

Charles Albert's outlook was embittered by the knowledge that Piedmont was looking forward to Victor Emmanuel's accession; in consequence the heir to the throne was kept in the background as much as possible, and subjected to all the slights consistent with the Royal prestige. It was undoubtedly good for him; it eradicated from his mind any illusions about divine right of kings or the sanctity of the Lord's anointed. He could give free rein to his military tastes at a time when the army of Piedmont was the only bulwark against Austrian aggression; practical soldiering gave him experience which proved invaluable later, when every political question which arose in Italy was indissolubly bound up with a military one. It was far more necessary that the future King should be able to estimate the chances of a campaign against Austria than that he should be an authority on Court etiquette. From Rienzi onwards Italy had found talkers enough; it needed a soldier to serve her turn.

Yet there was one of the principal traits of his father's character which Victor Emmanuel inherited —or it may have been the result of environment rather than heredity. Brought up in a Court impregnated with the atmosphere of sybilline nuns and prophetic father confessors, it was perhaps inevitable that Victor Emmanuel should be superstitious. But he was unlike his father in that he did not allow his superstitions to interfere with his policy. When there was no question of policy he seems to have given freer rein to his superstitious tendency.

Some of the stories told about him are interesting although they are probably untrue; they certainly smack of having been devised to fit known facts. Thus it is said that he was anxious to help Napoleon III in 1870 (he *did* display a hankering for this policy) because a prophecy stated that the same day would see the end both of Napoleon's power and of his own. As it happened, the oracle was truly

Delphic. Napoleon III died January 9th, 1873, and Victor Emmanuel died January 9th, 1878.

Another prophecy, already alluded to, declared that Rome would be fatal to him; a more particular version even went so far as to say that he would not survive his first night in the city. It seems to have influenced Victor Emmanuel's actions to some extent. Rome fell to his armies in September, 1870, but he displayed little eagerness to enter his new capital. Perhaps he wanted to spare Pius's feelings as much as possible; perhaps he had a lingering fear that France might still be victorious over Germany and return to drive him out again. However it was, he kept away from Rome until late in December, when the flooded Tiber threatened to ruin the whole city, and the waters were washing up corpses against the façade of the Palazzo Borghese. Then the appeals of his officials overcame his reluctance, and he rode into the city. But he came late at night, and he left early the next morning, having been hardly four hours in the city. He did not allow his first night in Rome very much opportunity of doing him harm. It was nearly six months later that he made his triumphal entry, and his first prolonged stay, and all his life he spent as little time as he could in Rome.

This might have been a mere natural result of his predilection for his native province, but the detractors make much of it. The sneer is typical, but perhaps it better serves the purpose of showing how little food there is for malicious gossip in the King's career.

As regards women, the case is a little different. The House of Savoy has earned a distinctive reputation for gallantry, and Victor Emmanuel, differing, as usual, from his father, went a long way towards sustaining it. Yet it must always be remembered that the Court of Italy, whether it were established in Turin, in Florence, or in Rome, never sank to

o

the depths habitual to that of Naples—nor, for that matter, could any comparison be drawn between the Courts of Victor Emmanuel and of Napoleon III.

The rumour ran that the King was not too particular in his amours. Perhaps he was not: indeed, it hardly seems likely that he was. It was more economical, to say the least, if he were not. Having regard for the precarious state of the national finances all through Victor Emmanuel's reign it was well that he had none of Napoleon III's tendency to lavish expenditure on women. But, above all, the most important point was that the King did not allow himself to be influenced by the women with whom he associated. There had been a dark period, between Novara and the Tchernaya, when the malcontents had hinted wildly that the King's pacific attitude towards Austria was due to the prejudices of his wife, Adelaide of Austria. At this period after the event it is easy to realize the absurdity of the rumour; Victor Emmanuel was no more pacific towards Austria than he had to be. It may even be stated quite definitely that Queen Adelaide would have had no more restraining influence in the event of war with Austria than the meanest voter in Piedmont. The death of Adelaide at the same time as the entry of Sardinia into the Crimean War put a stop to the rumours; and perhaps it was as well for Italy that the Queen did die. It relieved the King of a certain amount of strain, and it made it easier for Italy to believe that he was absolutely Italian in his sympathies.

Apart from Adelaide, and disregarding the many women who held his attention for a time (hardly any of them could boast of more than a month's favour), there was one woman who could fairly claim to have been mistress of his heart. That was Rosina, later Countess of Mirafiori. Her title came to her late in life; she was not of noble origin.

Rather the contrary, for Rosina (all Italy came

to know her as Rosina) was the daughter of one of the Sardinian Royal Guard. Unbelievable as it may seem, it was by accident that she attracted Victor Emmanuel's attention, but it was an accident that bore considerable fruit. While Adelaide lived, the affair was conducted with some circumspection. Rosina's father was quieted with a commission and a small pension, and Rosina was installed in one of the Royal châteaux outside Turin. There is a legend to the effect that Queen Adelaide once met one of Rosina's children, took him in her arms, and treated him with great affection (a rather similar story is told of the Empress Josephine's meeting with the King of Rome), but the legend is based on less than hearsay. However, after Adelaide's death, and especially after the conquest of Lombardy and Naples, the attachment between Victor Emmanuel and Rosina was displayed quite publicly—at least, it was given as much publicity as the King cared for, which is saying little.

Several children were born of the union; it was a fact which sanctified it in the eyes of the Italian public rather than the reverse. Under the Bourbon régime in Naples the illegitimate birthrate was hardly lower than the legitimate, so that the Royal acknowledgment of the family went no way towards lessening the Royal popularity.

Rosina was an unambitious woman. She had no desire to rule a Court, or to cut a figure in the eyes of the public. She disliked living anywhere except in Piedmont. She was hardly interested even in fashions. The people of Turin were used to seeing her in her box at the theatre, dowdily dressed except for her magnificent jewels, but she rarely accompanied Victor Emmanuel when he visited the rest of his kingdom. It was largely for this reason that the King disliked living out of Piedmont—and it was perhaps because of this that constitutional government was given a fair chance of developing in Rome.

After the death of Queen Adelaide, Rosina became Countess of Mirafiori (the name of a farming estate which Victor Emmanuel conferred upon her), and her children, as they grew up, entered the government service. But it was upon his recovery from the serious illness which had threatened his life soon after the capture of Rome, that Victor Emmanuel took the decisive step. He made Rosina his wife, and her children legitimate in the eyes of the Church.

It was a deed which caused ill-concealed amusement in France and elsewhere, where the newspapers quoted unpleasant proverbs concerning the marriage of a mistress, but it was looked upon as a kindly act throughout Italy. Rosina, for her negative virtues, was beloved by the Italians, and Victor Emmanuel's marriage to her was considered very right and proper. The French prejudice was not so widespread in Italy, and moreover the ceremony had considerable political significance, in that it showed that the King had no objection to submitting to the law of the Church. Victor Emmanuel, after all his victories, settled down to a comfortable middle-age (he was only fifty-eight when he died) in his country seat of Mandria, close to Turin. The Court here was represented by half a dozen equerries and aides-de-camp, and Victor Emmanuel guarded his privacy by enclosing several square miles of land within a single high wall—probably the most extravagant act of his economical existence. It was against tourists—French, English and German—that he had to guard. The Italians had too much respect and affection for their monarch to intrude upon his privacy.

When their ideal, humdrum union was brought to an untimely end by the King's sudden death in Rome, Rosina was lying seriously ill at Mandria, and she did not long survive him. But her family has endured. The name of Mirafiori is still an honoured one in Italy, and a morganatic offshoot of the House of Savoy still holds commands and benefices in the peninsula.

The temptation to label the Countess of Mirafiori as the " Maintenon of Italy " is almost too great to be withstood. But such an appellation would be misleading. The achievements of the two women are as different as their careers are similar. Not once did Rosina meddle in State affairs. There is no black mark against her, no revocation of the edict of Nantes, no incitement of a Waldensian persecution. If there were any reason to believe Victor Emmanuel as susceptible to petticoat influence as was Louis XIV, Italy would owe much to the Countess of Mirafiori for her self-restraint.

However, it is quite certain that nothing save good reasons would ever divert Victor Emmanuel from any course which he believed to be the best. It was because of his acute perception of all the possibilities that lay in the revolt of the Duchies and Romagna that he was able to acquiesce without damaging argument in Napoleon III's decision to halt his army in mid-career at Villafranca, at a time when even Cavour turned against him and rated him as a time-server and a poltroon. It is probably to his steadfastness on that occasion that Italy owes her union; for Sardinia to have continued the struggle single-handed against Austria was to precipitate disaster. 1860, instead of finding three-quarters of Italy under the rule of Victor Emmanuel, might well have found the entire peninsula under Austrian suzerainty, and the House of Savoy dethroned and exiled. Or Humbert might have succeeded to the throne after a second Novara—and it is fairly certain that he was not of the stuff of which Victor Emmanuels are made.

Yet it is conceivable that Victor Emmanuel would have made the rash attempt, deeming it better for Italy that she should try and fail than that she should try and meet with half a success, had it not been for the fact that he foresaw the later developments in the Italian situation. He could make Napoleon serve Italy's turn (against his will and better judgment) whether the latter fought or not. He saw that nothing short of military force could tear the Duchies and Romagna from him, and he saw that Napoleon could not employ military force in this case, and that he would be compelled to counterbalance Austrian intervention. Despite Cavour's defection, Victor Emmanuel carried the matter through with a keenness of perception and a dexterity of finesse which must rank him in the very first flight of diplomatists.

Attention has already been drawn to the fact that if praise is given to Cavour for the policy associated with his name, at least as much praise must be given to Victor Emmanuel. For Cavour could never have carried out any of his schemes without the Royal approval, and in some cases (the entry into the Crimean War, for instance) without the assistance of the utmost influence the King could bring to bear. In those early days of representative government the responsibility was at least as much the King's as it was the Minister's; Cavour stood to lose only his office, Victor Emmanuel to lose his throne. It has been the fashion to look upon Victor Emmanuel as a rather simple soul, as indebted to Cavour at least as much as was Louis XIII to Richelieu, but the comparison is quite faulty. In the matter of Villafranca; in the estimation of Garibaldi's motives and character; in the calculation of the chances in the event of a war with France, Victor Emmanuel's judgment was correct, and Cavour's (there is no denying it) was incorrect.

And after Cavour's death, until the chances of party strife brought Crispi into power, Victor Emmanuel stood head and shoulders above any other Italian in office. It was undoubtedly the King who foresaw the victory of Prussia in the approaching Six Weeks' War, and it was the King who arranged the alliance with Prussia which won for Italy Venetia and the Iron Crown. It is doubtful if Prussia would have been victorious—or at least it is doubtful if she would have gained so crushing a victory—if Italy had not participated. Had Benedek had another hundred thousand men at his disposal, to say nothing of the advice and example of the Archduke Albert in addition, it is possible that von Moltke might have been beaten in Bohemia. And in that event Austria would have assumed the suzerainty of Germany, and Venetia would have remained in her hands. The compensation on the Rhine for which Napoleon clamoured would have been perforce accorded, and the war of 1870 might have been Franco-Austrian instead of Franco-Prussian. This struggle might have brought Italy Venetia, or it might have brought her Rome; it certainly could not have brought her both, and most probably it would have brought her neither, seeing that almost for certain she would have sided with France, and that France would almost for certain have been beaten.

Where Victor Emmanuel was at fault was that he did not take command in person of the armies of Italy in 1866. Cialdini and La Marmora were both good men; they both had had extensive experience of command in the field and they both had the prestige of victories (the Tchernaya and Castel-fidardo), but they were enemies politically. The condition, almost inevitable in a new State, that generals must also be politicians, was a deadly handicap. Cialdini was only human, not disinterested. Were La Marmora to gain a victory, the prestige he would acquire would root him in office for a generation to come, and would utterly blight the prospects of the political advancement of Cialdini and his friends. So Cialdini hung back, and did not accord to La Marmora even the little support he could have given, hampered as he was both by the strategic situation (with the Quadrilateral between the armies) and by civilian instructions. La Marmora moved forward to honourable failure at Custozza. It was the result that was to have been expected of an arrangement that sent the Prime Minister and a prominent member of the Opposition to command the two halves of the army of Italy.

But it seems probable that the fact that La Marmora, for the immediate good of Italy, consented to Cialdini's promotion to the supreme command after Custozza, saved Cialdini from the fate meted out to Ramorino after Novara. He would have deserved it.

With Victor Emmanuel in command the result of the campaign might have been different. It is hardly likely that Cialdini would have dared to disobey him. Only a very little more—the absence of a single brigade of Albert's army, or a little more keenness of vision on the part of the Italian higher command—would have turned the scale at Custozza in favour of Italy.

The possible consequences seem too vast to contemplate. Victory at Custozza would have handed over all Venetia to the Italians; it would have made Garibaldi's Tyrolese campaign more fruitful; it would have rendered possible an energetic advance into Austria. The armistice of Nikolsburg would have found Italy firmly established at Trent, and, by the terms of the original alliance, the Trentino would have passed to her. Napoleon, raging impotently on the other side of the Alps, could have been disregarded by a victorious Italy. The irredentist party in Italy would have been left with small grounds for argument. In that case, fifty years later, Italy's treaty engagements might have carried her into the war in 1914 as an ally of Austria and Germany, with results almost incalculable. On land Italy might have done little harm—the French Alps should have proved as impassable a barrier as were the Austrian ones, and the French and English divisions which rebuilt the Italian line after Caporetto could as easily have flung back the Italians from Mont Blanc—but by sea Italy could have come near to ruining the cause of England. The Italian and Austrian navies, with the *Goeben* and *Breslau* in the line as well, could have challenged the Entente's supremacy in the Mediterranean. Submarines based on Genoa and Leghorn would have worked much more havoc than those which pushed out from Pola or toiled down the Channel and past Gibraltar, especially as they would have been backed by a fleet in being of three times the strength of that of Austria. A victory by Italy at Custozza in 1866 might have won the war for Germany in 1918. The digression is surely excusable.

Yet there were several potent reasons against Victor Emmanuel's assumption of the supreme command in the field in 1866. La Marmora was undoubtedly a more experienced soldier; save for Victor Emmanuel's privilege of birth, he was his senior in the army; the popular opinion was that he was the greater soldier. For a King to command in the field might be regarded as unconstitutional— and to Victor Emmanuel the constitution was sacred. There might have been other considerations as well. The Quadrilateral was a tough nut to crack, and the Archduke Albert was a general of proved ability. Victor Emmanuel had no desire to go the same road as Charles Albert, and a defeat and a second forced abdication might have imperilled the dynasty. It must be remembered that the dynasty was Italy at that time; party factions and provincial jealousies had left the country with no other binding link. Most probably it was canny foresight on the part of Victor Emmanuel which saw to it that the blame of Custozza rested on other shoulders than his own.

To Victor Emmanuel, too, must be given the

credit for acquiescing in Garibaldi's organization of
the thousand and departure for Marsala. Assuredly
the credit is not Cavour's. The latter distrusted both
Crispi and Garibaldi, and refused them all countenance when they approached him in December, 1859.
Yet the expedition could not have been organized,
and most certainly could not have started, without
benevolent neutrality, to say the least, on the part
of the government. It must have been Victor
Emmanuel who overbore Cavour's objections. It
could have been no one else, and in the end it was
only a grudging approval that Cavour gave to the
filibustering expedition. So that it is to Victor
Emmanuel as much as to Garibaldi or Crispi that
Italy owes the conquest of Sicily and Naples. Mazzini
it may have been who heated the iron, Cavour may
have held it, and Garibaldi may have wielded the
sledgehammer, in the welding of Italy, but it was
Victor Emmanuel who made the welding possible,
who chose Cavour and Garibaldi for their duties,
who seized the tongs when Cavour's grip failed,
and who dealt many shrewd sledgehammer blows
himself.

Nevertheless, when all is said and done,
the greatest asset Italy possessed during Victor
Emmanuel's reign was his honesty. At a time when
vindictive party politics reduced honesty in government circles to its lowest possible ebb, and when the
manœuvres and counter-manœuvres of Napoleon III
and Bismarck dealt a mortal wound to international
morality, Victor Emmanuel's good faith was an
oriflamme to his people. After Novara he could
have abrogated the new constitution. By that act
he could have lightened the burden of defeat, and
so gained some support; Austria would have been
only too glad to have assisted; the Church and the
reactionary Conservatives would have rallied gratefully round him. That one single act would have
given him at once arbitrary power and justification

for it. It was the dream of Augustus, of Napoleon,
of George III. He refused to realize it.

Because of his constancy in this early trial, the
people of the Duchies, of Lombardy and of Venice
consented to submit themselves to him later. They
put aside the thoughts which had once possessed
them of establishing republics or separate limited
monarchies, with clumsy and elaborate constitutions;
they did not join him for the mere purpose of
obtaining a protector against Austria; they preferred
the rule of Victor Emmanuel to any other possible
form of government because they knew that he would
act in their interests and would never betray his
trust. It was more than they did for Charles Albert,
for Charles Albert had forfeited all confidence by his
apostasy during 1821-47.

So virtue was not only its own sole reward.
Later, Garibaldi held in his hands the future of
Naples and Sicily. He had elaborate plans for their
political education; the temptation must have been
severe that he should retain the power and supervise
the development of these plans himself. Francis'
offer of two millions sterling and alliance must have
shown him (if he did not realize it already) the extent
of his own personal influence. Yet when Victor
Emmanuel came forward, and declared that in his
opinion it would be best for Italy if Garibaldi were
to lay down his power and hand over the Two
Sicilies, Garibaldi believed him and did so. He knew
that personal interest alone would not induce the
King to make such a suggestion. And he knew that
however much the King's plans for the political
future of the Neapolitans differed from his own they
would be honestly devised and honestly acted upon.

The next year came what might well have been
a disaster for the infant kingdom. The two great
men of Italy, Victor Emmanuel and Garibaldi,
fell out. The battle of Aspromonte was fought,
Garibaldi was wounded, Italians shed Italian blood

as in the worst days of the Bourbon régime. Garibaldi loudly declared, in the heat of the moment, that Victor Emmanuel had betrayed him. It was a crisis in Italian history. But it was a crisis that passed. Even the mystified Garibaldists could not believe that the King had acted dishonestly. Garibaldi could have found no following had he started out to avenge Aspromonte, and he, too, soon came to realize that, whoever were guilty of treachery, it was not Victor Emmanuel. The King's reputation saved Italy from civil war.

There followed the long period of waiting for some turn in the situation which would leave Rome open to them. Garibaldi chafed at the inaction. He could fight and he could plot, but he could not wait —thereby just missing perfection. He believed the King's caution was due to timidity instead of common sense. He had no compunction at all about trying to force the King's hand—in his opinion kings were sent on to this world to have their hands forced. It must be remembered that Garibaldi was only a recent and partial convert from republicanism. He had a large following, who would obey him blindly, despite the fact that his last two expeditions had ended in disaster at Aspromonte and Sarnico.

Under these conditions he resolved to win Rome for Italy in spite of herself, in much the same fashion as the man who told his snivelling child, out on a day's holiday, that he would give him a sound thrashing and *make* him enjoy himself. It has already been told how his preparations split the Italian cabinet and paralysed the executive at the very moment when he was ready to start. All Victor Emmanuel could have done at that moment was to proclaim martial law and stop Garibaldi by main force on his own responsibility. It would have involved the employment of unconstitutional measures against a popular hero. He had done it once, but he could not do it twice. It would have exasperated Garibaldi sufficiently to start civil war. The only way to convince Garibaldi that Rome could not yet be Italy's was to let him try to take the city. If he failed, he would be convinced. If by any chance he succeeded, well and good. Garibaldi was allowed to start for Rome—via Mentana.

The circumstances were sufficiently involved to justify a suspicion that the King had arranged the affair with Napoleon III, for the purpose of teaching Garibaldi a lesson. Had Victor Emmanuel had behind him the record of Ferdinand II or of Napoleon, that suspicion would have been both intense and dangerous; as it was it was put aside by all except those Garibaldists who were blinded with disappointment. There was no new rupture in the State; the main body of the public trusted Victor Emmanuel so implicitly that the only prestige lost was the greater part of Garibaldi's.

Instances of Victor Emmanuel's value to Italy could be multiplied indefinitely. The man who had most influence over Venice before its incorporation in Italy was Manin, the last of the Doges, who had proclaimed Venice's independence in 1848, and who had held Venice against Austria for a whole year, until after Novara. Manin began as a Republican —an aristocratic Republican, as became a Venetian— and he had proffered alliance—not submission—to Charles Albert. But in after years, as an exile in Paris, he had come to realize that the best hopes for Venice's future lay in her becoming part of Victor Emmanuel's Kingdom of Italy. He had the moral courage to say so, and to admit that the separatist policy he had encouraged in 1848-49 was dangerous and unpatriotic. His opinions carried enormous weight in Venetia, and it was this pronouncement of his that finally decided Venice to cast in her lot with Victor Emmanuel. Manin would never have made the declaration had he not had the fullest confidence in the King, and he was a shrewd

judge of character. If the government of Italy had
rested solely in the hands of men like Rattazzi and
Menabrea he would never have come to this decision,
and Italy might have found herself eternally crippled
through the presence of an oligarchic Republic,
necessarily suspicious, and probably anti-Italian, on
her north-eastern frontier.

There is no denying the fact that Italy could be
only united under one *man*, not under one government. Garibaldi might have done it, but the fate
of Italy after his death would have been unenviable.
A military dictatorship without the prestige of a
dynasty behind it would have gone the way of the
South American dictatorships. And had the Powers
of Europe eventually stepped in to restore order they
could hardly have done anything very different from
what they did in France in 1814—restored the old
dynasties. Austria, at least, would not have been
averse to such a policy. Division would have been
inevitable. The south could tolerate a Piedmontese
monarch of the calibre of Victor Emmanuel, but they
would not have borne for one moment a Piedmontese
President who owed his power to parliamentary
intrigues.

So everything depended upon the King, plain,
simple, easy-going Victor Emmanuel, with his taste
for chamois hunting in the Alps, and his little
mercenary affairs with casual lights of love, and his
domestic passion for his Rosina, and his liking for
fried onions. Nothing flamboyant about him at all,
no talk about " baptisms of fire," not even a stray
telling phrase or two about " blood and iron," no
international exhibitions, no white horse and glittering staff and appeals to " forty centuries," no tame
buzzard trained to perch on his shoulder (to eat bacon
out of his hat), only a mind as keen as a razor and an
honesty as transparent as crystal.

Panegyric is a difficult art; the reader's mental
palate can be subtly and steadily stimulated if the

biographer can do the reverse instead, and make an Aunt Sally of his victim; if the writer laboriously builds up a few arguments in favour of his subject and then knocks them down with an epigram and an innuendo he is credited with sincerity and a sense of justice, and it really does very little harm to the memory of the man he is writing about. But unstinted praise does little good and some harm— especially as the available amount of praise is definitely limited and cannot be allotted to one man without detracting from the achievements of another.

But Victor Emmanuel, had he been able to foresee what would be written about him after his death, would have been perfectly satisfied that the credit of his achievements should be given to others as long as the achievements themselves remained.

CHAPTER XVI

AFTERWARDS

AT the death of Victor Emmanuel the Kingdom of Italy had been in existence only seventeen years; Venetia had been Italian for less than twelve, and Rome less than eight. Yet the achievement was complete. Like Minerva, sprung fully armed from the head of Zeus, Italy had sprung from the welter of Italian disunion equipped with all the necessities, a constitution, a dynasty, a history, and the second oldest order of chivalry in existence. It only remained to be seen whether the constitution would be a help or a hindrance, whether the dynasty would remember the history, and the Knights of the Annunciation their responsibilities.

Pius was dead. He only survived the death of his rival by a month, and the longest recorded tenure of the Papacy came to its gloomy close. For a brief space fortune seemed to smile on Italy. There was some talk of electing the new Pope on some more congenial soil, but the Ministry was overeager to pluck this thorn from Italy's side. The Cardinals revoked their decision, and a new prisoner was elected for the Vatican. Pius was borne to his grave amid the prayers of the faithful and the hoots of those who had suffered under him; the rioting along the line of route was hardly in the best of taste, perhaps, but it was in an atmosphere of rioting, active or suppressed, that Pius had passed his best days.

KING HUMBERT I

With Pius gone, and no cloud on the international horizon, and freed from the influence of a King who could overbear political extravagances, the politicians could now enter into the business of politics in the manner for which their souls yearned. They could build railways, when they were in power, in strategic situations—strategic from the point of view that they would win a few votes in doubtful districts. They could expand the numbers of the army so that more of their friends could be accommodated with comfortable administrative appointments or promotion to general's rank. They could arrange alarming crises in the House so that they could speculate profitably during the resultant uncertainty on the Stock Exchange. They could hold up Currency Bills so that the banks which their friends owned would not lose their valuable yet dangerous privileges. They could hound into retirement the most distinguished of their number—Crispi, who paid for an early indiscretion indulged in during the dark days of the Bourbon régime by losing office on a charge (unfounded) of bigamy. Transformism, only hinted at under Victor Emmanuel, dissolved the executive into a loose heterogeneous confederation of ineffective units.

The Irredentist party sprang to life under the spur of party needs. Misunderstanding with Austria was risked for the sake of a vote-catching appeal. Transformism resulted in indecision of policy. Indecision meant ineffectiveness, and led, almost inevitably, to corruption and to maladministration comparable to that of the Bourbons and the Hapsburg-Estensi. Uncomprehendingly Ministry after Ministry watched France's colony on the other side of the Mediterranean swelling and expanding, thanks to the stream of Italian migrants who poured thither from the troubled South. One Ministry saw Tunisia fall like a ripe plum into the eager hands of the French. Its hesitation was deservedly requited

P

by extinction, but the next flinched before France's
threat of war and left Egypt solely to England.
Taxation grew ever more burdensome as armaments
increased and the widening of the government under-
takings gave more scope for the peculators, but
only occasionally did revenue balance expenditure.
Financial crisis followed financial crisis; paper money
wobbled distressingly in its value compared to gold,
and the government stocks constituted a highly
speculative form of investment—which was well for
the speculators in touch with the government.

Brigandage in the South recrudesced; in Sicily
the secret societies had their grip on the throat of
the Press and their fingers in every pie; Camorristi
and Mafiusi were alternately in league and at feud,
with unhappy results for Italy in either event.

Eventually Crispi fought his way back to office.
For a time matters improved. The budgets balanced
both in fact and in theory. On his accession to office
he found that Italy, with the secret approval of
France, had, two years before, seized a fragment of
Africa in the hope of developing an Italian Empire.
There had been mismanagement there as elsewhere;
the Ministry that had dispatched the first troops
thither had confidently expected them to push steadily
through to the Nile, regardless of the difficulties of
the country, of the opposition of the Abyssinians,
and of the power of the Mahdi. Crispi substituted
a policy of steady expansion for one of hare-brained
optimism. Money, painfully saved from other
departments, was poured out like water over the
barren province. Twenty thousand men were needed
to hold the province down and to ensure against
attacks from Abyssinia. In the hope of stimulating
a wholesome civil war in Abyssinia which would
leave Eritrea in peace, Crispi supported a pretender
to the throne—a sound policy, but unfortunately
the actual monarch perished in battle against the
Mahdists, and Menelik reached the supreme power

too easily and, perforce, with the official approval of
Italy.

For a space a spasmodic coalition of Right and
Left hurled Crispi from office, but no coalition could
hope to act as vigorously as the situation called for.
A year of office saw the coalition in fragments. A
frightful financial crisis, resulting in the failure of the
largest bank in Italy and the shaking of Italian credit
all over the world brought ruin to thousands, and
distress was widespread all over the peninsula.
Disappointed office-seekers and rabid Republicans
stirred up trouble everywhere. Sicily and Tuscany
and Romagna rose in revolt. The rebellion was only
extinguished after considerable bloodshed by Crispi,
who returned to office in answer to appeals from all
sides. He had a nearly hopeless task before him.

His economical administration of the public
services brought upon him the enmity of the King,
who found that it made it more difficult for him to
find profitable places for his friends. The Church
hated him as a free-thinker and an old Garibaldist.
The Left and the Right, although discredited, bided
their time to attack him at a disadvantage. Crispi
was an Anglophile, and openly declared that when an
opportunity arose he would break with the Triple
Alliance and attach himself to England for the sake
of the Italian possessions in Africa. In consequence
Germany and Austria turned against him, and as he
supported England in her Mediterranean policy,
which was opposed to that of Russia and consequently
to that of France, all the influence of these two
Powers was brought to bear against him as well.
All these enemies had their share in pulling Crispi
from power.

The King steadily opposed all Crispi's suggestions
for the remodelling of the army in Eritrea.
Apparently out of sheer spite he postponed the
recall of Baratieri, the hopelessly incompetent Italian
commander-in-chief there. In the Armenian crisis

of 1895 Crispi was pledged to support England by arms if necessary. The reinforcements which ought to have been sent to Massowa had to be held back in case need arose for their employment in Asia, and Italy had not the money to equip another force— nor was another force available, thanks to much maladministration. France and Russia, exasperated by Italy's support of England, incited Menelik of Abyssinia to attack the Italian provinces in Eritrea. French rifles were adroitly run ashore on the Red Sea coast and found their way into the hands of Menelik's fierce tribesmen. Baratieri, in command at Massowa, heard that the King had at last consented that Baldissera should replace him. He determined to strike a blow for fame while he had yet time. Crispi had counselled discretion and a moderation of activity; Baratieri risked everything upon one decisive blow. The Abyssinians outnumbered his force by six to one; they knew the country thoroughly; there were innumerable strong positions which they could take up; they had spies in every Italian camp, and they were led by Menelik, who had all the fierce cunning of the fighting tribesman.

Twice Baratieri met with slight but galling reverses, and in the end he determined on a night attack. He could have thought of nothing more suicidal. A night attack over the most difficult country in the world, with badly trained troops, disheartened and badly supplied and hampered by extreme ignorance of the country, against an enemy who had learned the art of desert and hill warfare at the hands of the Soudanese, was bound to fail. Baratieri would have been lucky had he only met with a reverse. As it was, he was unlucky, and met with disaster. Half his force was annihilated, and the other half was badly cut up. Out of fifteen thousand men Baratieri lost six thousand killed and four thousand taken prisoner.

Crispi fell from power, and the exultant Right

seized once more on office. Baratieri was court-martialled and dismissed. He was not shot—he had done the new government too good a turn for that, and he had too many friends in high places. Besides, now that Crispi was gone there was no object to the government mind in raking up the unsavoury past. In fact, such a proceeding would have been distinctly unpleasant.

The victors contented themselves merely with reversing the entire policy of the preceding party. They repudiated Crispi's agreements with England, published the confidential correspondence involved, and threw themselves heart and soul once more into the Triple Alliance. The shiftiness of Italian policy became more and more deplorable. A foreign policy dependent upon a parliamentary majority is always untrustworthy; when that policy is dependent upon a majority in a parliament given over to transformism it must necessarily be untrustworthy beyond description.

And now that parties were vanishing, now that Republicans accepted monarchical forms, now that the Right pressed for extension of the franchise because that would give them more votes proportionately, while the Left opposed the measure for that reason, now that extreme Left and extreme Right coalesced to ensure the downfall of the Centre, a new party began to develop and to bid fair to outnumber the tiny groups opposed to it.

For they were opposed to it. They all turned upon it with an indignation and a hatred surpassing that with which they had regarded the Republicans in the old days. The very name was alarming. Socialist deputies were beginning to appear in the Chamber. Already powerful trades unions had begun to appear in the industrial North, and had won strike after strike against the unorganized employers, and now their profound political influence was flung into the scale on the side of the Socialist party.

Despite the fact that they represented all shades of thought the Socialists were a solid enough party in the House, and the only party to compare with them in numbers or solidity was that of the Catholic reactionaries. The result was that every deputy who was not a Socialist rallied under the banner of this other section. Yet even then they were hardly strong enough to destroy the Socialist party with the strong hand, and the time-honoured procedure of bribing the electorate with extravagant public works was continued. Tentative reaction was masked by enormous expenditure of public money. The expenditure was met (as far as it was met at all) by grinding taxation, and, as evasion was simpler and cheaper than payment in consequence of the disorder of the revenue departments, the taxation tended to be heavier than ever and to press with greater stringency upon the classes who could not evade—in other words, upon the poorer classes. It is hardly surprising that the unrest grew more and more intense.

The Socialist party, as already mentioned, comprised people of all shades of opinion. From mere advanced radicalism they tended towards federal republicanism, and beyond that to revolution and anarchy. In the ranks of the anarchists was found an Italian to attempt a deed which would set the seal upon the policy of the extreme Socialist wing.

Humbert's popularity had waned steadily all through his reign. When he came to the throne his reckless bravery at Custozza and his sincere charity had won him a position in the affections of the Italians second only to that of Victor Emmanuel himself. But as the years went by, and the scandal of maladministration grew worse, he lost this position rapidly. Not unfairly (seeing that his influence had maintained the General in command), Baratieri's disaster at Adowa was attributed to him, and the

army began to turn against him.   He could do little
to restore order in the prevailing chaos of parties; he
had no Cavour at hand to rule the turbulent deputies.
This last may have been his fault—it is impossible
that in the whole Chamber there was no man to suit
his purpose.   He simply failed to find him; perhaps
he did not look very hard.   Crispi would have served,
but Humbert could not employ Crispi without
continual friction, and the economical administration
of the public revenues upon which Crispi insisted was
not to Humbert's taste.   He—or his friends—
intrigued against Crispi with disastrous results, and
the government was flung back into the chaos of
transformism from which it could only be rescued
by the Catholic party.   There was no one left with
any interest in the King; he was not an asset to any
party.

Under these circumstances appeared Bresci, the
anarchist; he would attempt that which even
Mazzini had been unable to find an Italian to do—
he would take the life of the King.   The deed was
done at Monza, in the heart of the industrial portion
of Italy, where Humbert with the courage of his
race exposed himself with a needless lack of
precaution.   He had had warning; a lunatic had
made the same attempt soon after Humbert had
come to the throne, and another Nihilist had done
so as well only three years before.   Bresci, of course,
paid the penalty, but there were many people who
owed him a debt of gratitude.   The political strife
had grown too chaotic and dangerous; the anti-
Socialists wanted a new figure-head—one which had
not been discredited by military disasters and
unsavoury scandals of all kinds; while the Nihilists
were in need of a deed that would rivet upon them
the attention of Europe.

To the perilous throne succeeded Victor
Emmanuel, Prince of Naples.   He took, perforce,
the title of Victor Emmanuel III; he could do

nothing else, seeing that his grandfather had been Victor Emmanuel II, but the title served to demonstrate the old theory that Italy was only a conquest and appanage of Piedmont, and the lesson was accentuated by the bestowal of the title of Prince of Piedmont on the heir to the throne.

With the approval of the new King, the anti-Socialists began to search for another policy with which to combat their opponents. It was a matter of vital necessity to Victor Emmanuel, who neither wanted to share the fate of his father nor that of Charles Albert. The old system of public works —*panem et circenses*—was abandoned, and some sort of attempt was made, in defiance of the vested interests involved, to grapple with the corruption of the public services and with the secret societies. But this was not enough. Something more striking had to be brought under public notice.

Austria had nearly served her turn. While the kingdom was young she had counteracted French influence, but now France was not so disposed to meddle with Italian affairs. Indeed, she was so engrossed with the menace of a growing Germany across the Rhine that she was not anxious to do anything that would offend her south-eastern neighbour in the slightest. The French Concordat with the Pope was obviously drifting to a speedy end, and clerical, anti-Italian influence was less noticeable. On the other hand there were several possibilities of dispute between Italy and Austria. The latter had kept possession of the Trentino, and this last province was undoubtedly Italian in sentiment—not as much, perhaps, as the Irredentist party claimed, but enough to cause continual soreness and friction. Then the Austrian coastland, too, had a large Italian element, while Austria displayed a tendency to expand along the Adriatic in a fashion disturbing to Italian Imperialists, who were beginning to cast longing eyes

VICTOR EMMANUEL III

on Albania, especially since the King, four years before his accession, had married a Princess of Montenegro.

In addition, there seemed undoubted proof that Italy was in need of colonies. Eritrea was too unhealthy and unproductive, while the Abyssinian menace was serious, and England disapproved on principle of the establishment of a European power on the Red Sea. Italian emigrants ignored Eritrea; instead they poured into Algeria (which French colony owed two-thirds of its immigrant population to Italy), into the United States, and into South America. Italian manufactures had reached a stage when it seemed highly desirable that there should be Italian colonies to purchase finished products and to send in exchange raw material.

The result of this was that the Liberals and Conservatives and the Clericals embarked on an Imperialist and, almost necessarily, anti-Austrian campaign in the hope of distracting public attention from internal affairs. The Irredentist movement received a great impetus. The Italian clamour for colonies began to make itself heard throughout Europe. It was a subtle stroke of policy. It enabled the anti-Socialists to brand the Opposition as unpatriotic and anti-Italian. So it was, to a large extent, but not nearly as much as the government party declared.

Early in the reign—in 1904—the anti-Socialists were forced into even firmer combination by the ominous growth of the Socialist party and the strongly supported threat of a general strike. At the first hint of such a move Right and Centre rushed into indissoluble amalgamation; the King was on their side, and the Clerical party, now fully alarmed, came over to him as well, despite the fact that since 1870 the Church had been opposed to the House of Savoy. The combination was very powerful; for the time the Socialist menace was neutralized, and the ministerialists were able to lead the people forward along the thorny road to Empire.

Naval and military administration was an Augean stable beyond the power even of Victor Emmanuel, talented and energetic as he was, to restore to purity, but some steps were made in this direction, and the annual deficits were gradually reduced to vanishing point. The next step was merely to find where best to employ this army and navy and credit balance.

There was now no corner left in the world in which some Power or other was not interested; the days when Italians had been able to possess themselves of Eritrea were long over. Some Power had to be fought; some others had to be consulted. Turkey was the weakest possible opponent, and on the other side of the Mediterranean, opposite Italy, there lay a Turkish province. Not much of a province, mainly desert, with oases few and far between, but at any rate something worth fighting for. France was agreeable—she was only too willing to have Italian attention taken from Algeria; England was agreeable—and England's agreement was very necessary, as she held the reins of power in Egypt, across which the Turkish armies must march if they came at all. Austria was agreeable; the Balkan problem was too involved for her to bring in another complication, and besides, Italy was her ally.

So a quarrel was picked with Turkey—anyone could pick a quarrel with Turkey; the Italian fleet bombarded the Tripoli forts, and twenty thousand Italians landed in Libya.

They had to work very hard for small profit. At the head of the Turkish resistance was a man of extreme talent—he who had lately been the leader of the movement which had brought Abdul the Damned from his throne, and who in after years was to make the name of Enver Pasha famous throughout Europe. By sea the Turks could do little, thanks to the

overpowering strength of the Italian navy; by land
England's refusal (received with vast indignation by
Turkey, but only to be expected) to allow the
Turkish armies to march across Egypt restricted the
possibilities of resistance very considerably. Nevertheless, the Turks and Arabs fought hard and
frequently with success. At Ain Zara the Italians
won a Pyrrhic victory; at Bir Tobias they were
beaten; but they went stolidly on with their task
of consolidating their power, helped by two bloody
victories at Zanzur and another at Derna. At last,
when the attitude of the Balkan alliance became
menacing, Turkey signed a reluctant peace.

She handed over Tripoli and Cyrenaica to Italy,
but it was a gift of a Nessus' shirt. The Arabs went
on fighting almost as though it was not their duty
to render obedience to a self-constituted authority,
and there were not wanting hints that they were
helped a little still by Turkey. Italy had to hand
back the Turkish islands—Rhodes and others—on
which she had laid greedy hands, and had the
mortification of seeing them fall at once into the
power of the victorious Greeks. All she had won
were the barren provinces of Libya, filled with
fanatical rebels. She could, and did, pour out money
in millions over the desert sands, but money cannot
buy a reliable rainfall. It cannot even make sure
of the allegiance of Arab tribesmen.

The war had some of its designed effect, although
a few full-blooded victories would have been desirable.
It checked to some extent the popularity of the
Socialists, and it was a powerful argument against
the disruptive federalism of the majority of that
party. Yet it led to all sorts of complications.
Germany, anxious for the alliance both of Italy and
Turkey in the approaching inevitable war, plunged
into hectic intrigues to create a party favourable to
herself. German capital and German emissaries
played havoc with the stability of the ministerial

party—although Socialism was the last thing that the German government wanted to favour. Moreover, the Irredentists, once given rein, were impossible to check, and maintained a violent anti-Austrian propaganda which boded ill for the continuance of the Triple Alliance. France held little that Italy could now covet (the Libyan expedition had exhausted Italian colonial ambitions), while Austria held Italian Tyrol and all the coastland. Moreover, Italy was becoming more and more ambitious as regards the Balkan Peninsula; there was an Italian element all along the Adriatic coast, and more than once Italy —either Venice or Napoleon's Kingdom of Italy— had ruled Austrian and Turkish territory; Napoleon had carried the Italian frontier as far as the border of Montenegro, while Venice once had ruled the Morea for a century. So the Irredentists had plenty of material to work upon, and their activities received a further impetus when it became clear that the conquest of Libya (even if Libya should ever be conquered) would not prove a salve for all the troubles of Italy.

The development of the Great War in 1914 from a Balkan quarrel in itself made it unlikely that Italy would assist Austria, especially as Italy was able to find in the terms of the treaty of alliance several loopholes of escape. The entry of England upon the French side settled the question. England could too easily kindle a flame of insurrection throughout the peninsula for the ministerialists to think of fighting France and England and the Socialists all at once merely to confirm Austria in the overlordship of the Balkans. Italy declared her neutrality, and at the same time made canny preparations to establish herself on the other side of the Adriatic.

Yet it was impossible for Italy to remain neutral. There was too much at stake altogether. If the Central Powers were victorious then Italy could abandon all hopes of the coastland and of influence in the Balkans. Besides, Turkey was Germany's ally. The flames of rebellion in Tripolitana were not even yet extinguished, and on the strength of that Turkey might well claim the recession of the province at the general peace. Moreover, mere neutrality would not secure for Italy, in the event of a victory for the Entente Powers, that position of predominance in the Adriatic for which she hungered. The Entente might perhaps, more to annoy Austria than to please Italy, toss her the Trentino, but they would hardly do more. Russia would see to that.

Above all, there was the need for Italy to pull herself together. She had need again of a common cause for all parties to work for, just as she had had in 1866. A big war would rally the people to the Ministerial side. And there were the Socialists to be considered. Only a month before the outbreak of the war the government party had to strain every nerve and sinew to overpower an attempt at a Socialist coup. If war were declared, the hands of the government party would be greatly strengthened. Socialist activities could then be denounced as treason, and a very powerful case could be made out against them in the eyes of the public. Obviously, there were sound reasons for the entry of Italy into the war.

That settled, it was easy enough to decide upon which side to intervene. The German plan of campaign had been wrecked on the Marne, and the battles of Ypres had beaten them off from the Channel ports. The Serbian victories seemed to show that the Austrians could be easily enough dealt with, and the Russian victories in the Caucasus and the collapse of the Turkish attempts against Egypt were a proof tnat Turkey was not to be feared. The King, of course, was definitely anti-Austrian; the glory of his house rested on a memory of victories over Austria, and would be sadly dimmed by the propaganda necessary if Italy were to become an ally

of Austria. A tradition of a century called for war
with Austria, and it seemed to the government that
Italian intervention would turn the scale in favour
of the Entente.

Austria, seriously alarmed, made offers of
territorial concessions, just as she had done in 1866.
Germany sent an ex-Chancellor and Foreign
Minister, Prince Bulow, in haste to Rome to try
to pacify the Italian interventionists. But the
Austrian offers were too small, and were severely
qualified by conditional clauses, while the Entente,
anxious for the safety of the Mediterranean in view
of the Dardanelles expedition, was profuse in its
offers of other people's belongings. The British
offers won the day, and war was declared on Austria
by Italy. But characteristically, German influence
was able to arrange that war was not similarly
declared on Germany, and this anomalous situation
was maintained for months.

As in 1866, the Italian armies, misdirected by
politicians, went plunging forward to defeat across
a strategically unfavourable frontier. The Austrians,
heavily outnumbered, fought desperately hard and
held up the Italian advance only a few miles within
Austrian territory. A year of fighting showed small
gains for Italy, and then the Austrians, granted a
breathing space by the Russians, struck back fiercely.
It was the story of Custozza over again. The Italian
line recoiled; Asiago and Asiero fell to the Austrians.
But no Novara followed. The Italians were able to
rally on the very verge of disaster, bad weather broke
up the Austrian attack, and the end of 1916 found
the battle line stabilized unsteadily, with Gorizia in
Italian hands. During the spring of the next year
Italian blood was poured out in streams to little
purpose. Effort followed effort, offensive succeeded
offensive, but the gains were small and the losses
enormous. One Ministry had already fallen—the
disasters on the Asiago plateau had been too much

for it—and another began to totter, although it had
made manly attempts to stiffen the spirit of the
administration, and had actually succeeded in carrying through a declaration of war against Germany.
But now the Russian revolution came to free the
hands of Austria and Germany.   German divisions
came secretly to the aid of the Austrians, and
German munitions were poured into Austria.   A
German general came to supervise the grand attack.

The blow fell late in 1917, and its effect was
enormous.   All the Italian gains were swept away
in the course of a few hours.   The Italian line was
forced back from ridge to ridge, from river to river,
till Venice was imperilled and it seemed as if a
few weeks would see the Germans in Rome.   Once
more the ministry fell, and with it this time
fell Cadorna, the commander-in-chief.   Ministerial
influence and high connections could no longer save
him, nor could the memory of his father (he was the
son of the general who took Rome in 1870).   Diaz
took his place, and to help him came French and
British divisions—some of them marched over the
Alps.   The losses had been immense.   More than
one Italian army corps, falling back to the
Tagliamento or the Piave, found that wild panic had
destroyed prematurely the bridges by which they had
hoped to pass, leaving them to be annihilated by the
pursuing Austrians.   It seemed as if this was the
Novara that Austria was expecting, but the precipitate Italian retreat had served one purpose at
least—it had got the Italians out of the way so that
succeeding Austro-German blows fell largely on
empty space.   The French and Italian divisions
steadied the line; the Piave was held, and the
Austrian offensive came to an end.   Christmas found
Venice still safe.

In 1918 an opportune flooding of the Piave ruined
the Austrian offensive of June (the weather was not
so kind to the Austrians as it was to the Germans in

France), and immediately afterwards the Italians counter-attacked. The motley horde, Italians, British, French, even Americans, met with swift success. The Austrian army was falling to pieces, thanks to steady propaganda on the part of the Allies and to four years of dwindling supplies; the Germans had been withdrawn to fend off Foch's great counter-offensive in France; six quiet months had restored the Italian army after the disaster of Caporetto.

The offensive began in late October; the Tenth Army (more than half British or American) burst across the Piave, and, vigorously supported on its flanks, pushed steadily towards the lost frontier. As the advance progressed the Austrian defence became more and more feeble. Fifty thousand prisoners were taken (a quarter of them by the Tenth Army) and the triumph of Vittorio Veneto left the Austrians helpless. They appealed for an armistice, and one was granted to them on terms reminiscent of the Old Testament in its severity. Austria had collapsed; the war was nearly over, and the Italians could congratulate themselves on having joined the right side. In the war her defeats were all her own; her victories were shared with troops of other countries.

It is a motif that runs throughout Italian history. Novara, the two battles of Custozza, Caporetto—all these were fought by Italians and were lost. Magenta, Solferino, the Tchernaya, Vittorio Veneto, were French or British victories as much as they were Italian. Verily can Italy be looked upon as fortunate.

The treaties of Versailles have been wittily described as " a peace with a vengeance." They gave Italy more than she asked for. In the dark days after Caporetto Italy had moderated her demands. She had abandoned her trans-Adriatic ambitions and had consented to the proposed forma-

tion of a Jugo-Slav state, but now in the flush of
victory she came to regret her rash promises. Italian
politicians at Versailles won for their country Italian
Tirol and the valley of the Adige, thereby giving
Italy a sound strategic frontier—and transferring the
Irredentist difficulty to the other side. Italian
public opinion would not tolerate the abandonment
of the whole coastland, and d'Annunzio's dash won
for her, in the teeth of Jugo-Slav disapproval, the
towns of Fiume and Zara. At last Italy could be
said to be complete.

A French-Austrian disagreement had won
Lombardy for her; a German-Austrian disagreement had won Venetia for her. A French-German
disagreement had won Rome for her, and now
another French-German disagreement had won Tirol
and Fiume for her. No Italian regiment bears on its
colours the names of Adowa or Custozza, but the
Italian flag waves in Venice and Massowa.

How that has come about it has been the purpose
of this book to tell. It is beyond its scope to
continue the story of Imperial Italy, or to tell of
the postwar Socialist troubles, and of Mussolini
marching on Rome to the strains of La Giovinezza.
The blackshirts rule in Rome and tyrannize over
Milan; the memory of Cavour's dictum that any fool
can reign by the aid of proclaiming a state of seige
has faded like the wreathes on Victor Emmanuel's
grave. Nor need it be asked how many of those
same turbulent blackshirts would have followed a
militant Socialist leader if one had arisen in time to
forestall the reactionary coup.

Be it as it may, Signor Mussolini has had given
to him an opportunity greater than any of those of
which Victor Emmanuel made such brilliant use.
Whether or not he will employ it; whether or not
a Charlemagne will arise from this new line of
Mayors of the Palace, time alone will show. Half
a lifetime—half Victor Emmanuel's lifetime—was

Q

sufficient to unite Italy. Yet even now, thanks to those who came after him, she is not yet fully compact. It is the duty of these new successors to see that the work is not undone to which the greatest man Italy has ever produced gave all his strength.

INDEX